Salesperson Motivation and Performance
A Predictive Model

Research for Business Decisions, No. 50

Gunter Dufey, Series Editor
Professor of International Business and Finance
The University of Michigan

Other Titles in This Series

No. 43 *The Auditor-Client Contractual Relationship: An Economic Analysis* Linda Elizabeth DeAngelo

No. 44 *Turnaround Strategies in the Commercial Banking Industry* Hugh Martin O'Neill

No. 45 *A Forecast for the Grocery Retailing Industry in the 1980s* James L. Brock

No. 46 *Multinational Accounting: A Research Framework for the Eighties* Frederick D. S. Choi, ed.

No. 47 *Valuation of Savings and Loan Associations* Philip W. Glasgo

No. 48 *Commercial Bank Underwriting of Municipal Revenue Bonds* Paul A. Leonard

No. 49 *Technological Innovation: The R & D Work Environment* Augustus Abbey

No. 51 *Stock Exchange Listings, Firm Value, and Market Efficiency* Gary C. Sanger

Salesperson Motivation and Performance
A Predictive Model

by
Nicholas Carlton Williamson

UMI RESEARCH PRESS
Ann Arbor, Michigan

Copyright © 1982
Nicholas Carlton Williamson
All rights reserved

Produced and distributed by
UMI Research Press
an imprint of
University Microfilms International
Ann Arbor, Michigan 48106

Library of Congress Cataloging in Publication Data

Williamson, Nicholas Carlton.
 Salesperson motivation and performance: a predictive model.

 (Research for business decisions ; no. 50)
 Revision of thesis (Ph.D.)–University of North Carolina at Chapel Hill, 1980.
 Bibliography: p.
 Includes index.
 1. Selling–Mathematical models. 2. Employee motivation–Mathematical models.   I. Title. II. Series.
 HF5438.25.W53 1982   658.3'044   82-4905
 ISBN 0-8357-1336-9   AACR2

Table of Contents

List of Tables   *ix*

List of Figures   *xi*

Acknowledgments   *xiii*

1 Introduction   *1*
    Vroom's Theory as a "Within-Persons" Model   *4*
    Measurement Issues in Research Using Vroom's Model   *5*
    Intrinsic and Extrinsic Rewards (Outcomes) and Vroom's Theory   *6*
    Job Scope, Job Challenge and "Need Achievement"   *6*
    Job Scope and Salesperson Motivation   *7*
    Participation, Job Challenge and "Need Achievement"   *7*
        Management by Objectives and Salesperson Performance   *7*
        Job Challenge   *9*
        A Comparison of Different Theories of Motivation   *10*
            Predictions of Vroom's Theory   *10*
            Predictions of Locke's Goal-Setting Theory   *11*
            Predictions of Atkinson's "Need Achievement" Theory   *11*

2 Literature Review   *15*
    Nature of the Study of Motivation   *15*
    Early Motivation Theories   *16*
        Scientific Management and Salesperson Motivation   *16*
        The Human Relations Movement in Management   *17*
    The Major Formal Theories of Motivation   *17*
        Skinner's Reinforcement Theory   *17*
        The "Drive Theory" of Hull   *18*
        The Field Theory of Lewin   *19*
    Process Theories of Motivation   *19*
        Equity Theory—J. S. Adams   *20*

vi   Table of Contents

        The "Expectancy" Theory of Vroom   21
            Problems Associated with Theory Misspecification   22
            Empirical Problems Related to the VIE Constructs   24
            The Model of Vroom as Representing Valid Thought Processes   25
            Variable Measurement Problems   25
            Managerial Application Problems   26
        Results of Formal Extensions of Vroom's Model   27
        Vroom's Model vs. Part II of the Research Model   27
    Content Theories of Motivation   28
        The Theory of Herzberg—"Satisfiers" and "Dissatisfiers"   28
        The "Need Hierarchy" of Motivation—Maslow   29
        The ERG Theory of Alderfer   29
        An Assessment of the Predictive Utility of "Need" Theories   30
    Atkinson, Steers and Locke   31
        The "Need Achievement" Theory of Motivation—Atkinson   31
        Research Done by Richard Steers   32
            Job Design and Work Motivation   32
            Task-Goal Attributes and Work Motivation   33
    Conclusion   34

3   Research Methods   35
    Sampling Procedure   35
    Data Collection Procedure   36
    Hypotheses to be Tested   38
    Constructs to be Measured and Scales to be Used   40
    The Performance Measures   44
        Span of Control of the District Manager   44
        Sales Territory Potential   44
        Sales Territory Dispersion   45
        Salesperson Experience   45
    Data Analysis   47
    Methodological Advances for Testing Hypothesis One   48
    Test of the Importance of Job Scope Issues   50
        Procedure for the Analysis   50
    "Participation" as a Predictor of Sales Performance   51
    Test of Hypothesis Four   52

4   Results   85
    Introduction   85
    Correlations Among the Constructs Used   85
        The Relationships Among the "n Ach" Scales and Performance   86
        The MPS Score and the Performance Variables   87

Table of Contents

        MPS and the Valence for Achieving the Company Goal   87
        The Performance Variables and the VIE Constructs   87
        Participation in Quota-Setting and Perceived Job Autonomy   88
        Intercorrelations among the Predictor Variables   89
    Scale Analysis   91
    Qualification of the Performance Variables   91
        The Sales Variable   91
        The Adjusted Sales Variable   92
        The Objective Performance Variable   92
    Results of the Tests of the Four Hypotheses   93
    Empirical Tests of the Four Hypotheses   95
        The Adjustment of the V and I Vars. by their Std. Devs.   99
        Discussion of the Results of the Hypothesis One Analyses   99
        The Effects of Job Scope on Sales Performance   101
        Discussion of the Results of Hypothesis Three Analyses   102
        Results of the Analyses Related to Hypothesis Three   103
        Discussion of the Results of Hypothesis Three   104
        Results of the Analyses Concerning Hypothesis Four   105

5   Summary, Implications and Suggestions for Further Research   111
    Summary of the Study   111
        Restriction of Range of Scores on "Need Achievement"   112
        Job Enrichment might not be Motivationally Salient   112
        "Need Achievement" and "Expectancy" as the ONLY Performance Predictors   112
    Management Implications   113
        "Need Achievement" and Sales Personnel Selection   113
        Management Programs and Salesperson Motivation   113
    Ideas for Further Research   113
        The Search for Useful Individual Difference Variables   114
        Develop Taxonomies of Job Outcomes   114

Appendix: Survey Materials   115

Bibliography   123

Index   129

List of Tables

1. Motivation and Performance Predictions   *11*
2. Research Design   *37*
3. Company Participation   *38*
4. Operational Definitions   *53*
5. Section Probing Job Outcomes   *54*
6. Choice of Important Job Outcomes   *58*
7. Instrumentalities of Attaining the Sales Quota   *59*
8. Instrumentalities of the Personal Goal   *62*
9. Scale for Job Scope Variables   *66*
10. Manifest Needs Questionnaire   *70*
11. The Jackson Preference Scale for "Need Achievement"   *74*
12. Task-Goal Attribute Questionnaire   *75*
13. Biographical Information   *78*
14. A Subjective Performance Assessment   *79*
15. An Objective Performance Assessment   *81*
16. Sales Volume Generated by Each Salesperson   *83*
17. End of Questionnaire   *84*
18. Overall Correlations among the Constructs   *86*

19. Correlations among the Performance and VIE Constructs   88

20. Correlation Matrix Using All Seventeen Job Outcomes   89

21. Correlations among the MPS and MBO Variables   90

22. Test of the Reliability of the Scales Used   91

22A. Pearson Product-Moment Correlation Matrix for the Objective Performance Variable and Potential Sources of Bias   93

23. Hypothesis One Regressions   96

24. Hypothesis One Regressions Using All Seventeen Job Outcomes   97

25. Correlations among the Valences and Outcomes   98

26. Formula for Adjusting the Valence Composite   99

27. The Motivational Potential Score and Performance   100

28. Hypothesis Two using Steers' Norms   101

29. MPS with the Expanded (I × V)   102

30. Results of the Analysis of Hypothesis Three   103

31. Results of Hypothesis Three Using Steers' Norm   104

32. Results of Hypothesis Three Using All Seventeen Job Outcomes   105

33. Preliminary Hypothesis Four Regressions   106

34. Test of the Equivalence of Regression Slopes-H4   107

List of Figures

1. A Model for Predicting Salesperson Job Performance   *12*
2. A Revised Model of Salesperson Performance   *113*

Acknowledgments

It is impossible to complete any undertaking of this magnitude without the contributions and support of many individuals. I am most indebted to Professor William D. Perreault, Jr. who was a major contributor at each stage of this research. His patience and energy in directing me in this endeavor were boundless. It is difficult to overestimate the benefit of the guidance which I have received from him both in his capacity as an outstandingly competent marketing researcher and also as a friend and teacher. I hope that I will be able to carry on the tradition of excellence in both research and teaching which he has demonstrated toward me.

My sincere appreciation is extended to Professors William J. Bigoness, Jay E. Klompmaker, James L. Littlefield and Frederick A. Russ for their sound advice and assistance.

I would also like to extend my sincere appreciation to the three companies (who wish to remain anonymous) and to their executive officers, sales managers and salespeople who gave their time and resources to this study.

Finally, I do now and will continue to give thanks to my wife, Beth, for her standing by me through the times of uncertainty which I experienced in the process of conducting this research. All of this would not have been possible without her love and patience.

1
Introduction

The theory of motivation which has received the most frequent use in making predictions of salesperson motivation and performance (Vroom, 1964) focuses upon the conditional availability of job outcomes as the main source of motivation to perform on the job and, as such, is inadequate for making predictions of salesperson performance in complex sales environments. Recent research in experimental psychology and organizational behavior suggests that knowledge of job scope (Steers and Spencer, 1977) and job challenge (Atkinson, 1958) variables, in conjunction with knowledge of the salesperson's need for achievement, will enable the salesforce researcher and sales management to predict with greater precision the salesperson's motivation and performance on the job.

This study describes in detail the variables which research in experimental psychology and organizational behavior has suggested will be of use in making job performance predictions, and their importance in making these predictions. In addition, methodological refinements in measurement and statistical manipulation of valence, instrumentality and expectancy (VIE) constructs are presented. A summary of the specific variables which have been investigated and methodological improvements which have been implemented is presented below.

1. A "between-persons" VIE model for predicting salesperson motivation and performance similar to that used by Galbraith and Cummings (1967), but one which has potential for overcoming the major problems which beset previous salesperson motivation research using "between-persons" VIE-based models is given and tested.

    a) Refinements into the measurement of the VIE constructs which are indicated as viable by similar research in the consumer attitudinal research literature are described.
    b) An expectancy construct which avoids the logical fallacy encountered in an assessment of the corresponding construct in the model by Galbraith and Cummings (1967) is given.

2. Job scope and "task-goal attribute" variables are introduced as variables which offer possible utility in increasing the concurrent job performance

prediction validities over that exhibited by research employing only Vroom's expectancy model or some variation thereof.

3. The predictive capabilities of the three main cognitive theories of motivation—those of Vroom, Atkinson and Locke—using a survey research design are assessed.

4. From a more broad-based point of view, an empirical determination of the general validity of the application of "job enrichment" and "Management by Objectives" (MBO) programs for sales management by conducting correlational studies relating job performance with job scope and "participation in quota-setting", respectively, is made.

Determining which variables affect a salesperson's motivation to perform on the job has in recent decades been of interest to sales researchers and sales management (Oliver, 1974; Churchill, Ford and Walker, 1976). The logic behind this interest is straightforward: knowing what motivates a salesperson to perform well on the job will enable sales management to adopt and follow policies that will cause the salesperson to function in a fashion that will be most profitable for the company.

Undertaking the study of the determinants of salesperson motivation and performance is a meaningful economic as well as philosophic exercise. Every year in the United States, many billions of dollars are spent on direct selling activities. Estimates indicate that corporate expenditures on direct selling activities are significantly larger than all corporate expenditures for advertising (Lucas, Weinberg and Clowes, 1975).

Salesperson motivation impacts corporate profitability in at least two different ways—both indirect and direct. A direct method is as described above: increased motivation to perform leads to greater effort, increased sales and, ultimately, higher profits (Oliver, 1974).

An indirect effect of salesperson motivation on company profits relates to the cost to the company of salesperson turnover. If a salesperson becomes dissatisfied with his job, then his job motivation and satisfaction levels may decrease sufficiently to cause him to go elsewhere for employment (or be terminated by management for related reasons). Hiring and training a new salesperson to replace the departed salesperson may cost the company a great deal of money (Churchill, Ford and Walker, 1974; Churchill, Ford and Walker, 1976; and Smyth, 1968).

From a larger perspective, the motivation to work is an issue at the heart of many of our economic maladies today. Motivation directly affects human productivity at work, and problems in the latter area are linked with increasing levels of inflation and a deteriorating standard of living.

For these and similar reasons, salesperson motivation is a topic of significant interest for research. With such sizeable interests invested by the company in the salesperson, one would expect that a substantial body of empirical research would have been undertaken to probe the determinants of salesperson motivation in depth. This is not the case, at least in the published literature. There are two reasons for the relative scarcity of empirical research in this topic in the past.

(1) Until very recently, salesperson aptitude, rather than salesperson motivation, has been the prime research focus in addressing methods of increasing salesperson productivity (Oliver, 1974). The assumption has been made that efforts to locate the most capable (rather than the most motivated) salesperson would be more fruitful. Research in this area, to date, has not been particularly promising, though (Cotham, 1970; Ghiselli, 1973). Cotham (1970) summarizes the dilemma in this area of research: "There is no single composite of qualities, each of specified strength, making up a complex entity called 'general sales ability'."

(2) Another reason for the dearth of published studies on salesperson motivation is that, until very recently, salespeople have been assumed to be motivated to perform primarily by money. The prevalence of this assumption in management thought is, in large part, due to the influence of the works of Frederick Taylor (Taylor, 1911) in the early part of the twentieth century. Taylor's work was based upon the premise that mankind is naturally lazy and that people work only to make enough money to live on. Most sales management textbooks prior to the 1970's have reflected this attitude by treating the topic of "salesperson motivation" as a subtopic of, or in tandem with, "salesperson compensation" (Davis and Webster, 1968; Stanton and Buskirk, 1969; and Still and Cundiff, 1969).

More recently written textbooks on sales management have suggested that issues other than "financial remuneration"—such as salesperson "need for Achievement", "need for Affiliation", and others—are important in motivating salespersons to perform on the job (Young and Mondy, 1978). However, no statement is made as to specifically which issues other than compensation are important in motivating the salesperson to perform on the job, and how these issues or variables interact in motivating the salesperson to perform.

The theory which has been used most frequently in salesforce research to predict salesperson motivation and performance is Vroom's expectancy theory of motivation (Vroom, 1964). Vroom's theory states that a person's motivation to perform on the job at a given effort level is a function of several variables symbolically stated below.

$$MF(j) = E(j)\Sigma_{i=1}^{r} I(ij) \times V(ij)$$

Where,
1. $MF(j)$ = the motivational force to exert a given level of effort, "j", to attain a goal under consideration.
2. $E(j)$ = expectancy of the successful attainment of the goal under consideration when level of effort "j" is exerted.

3. I(ij) = the correlation that successful goal attainment is perceived to have with experiencing the "i"th outcome, given that effort level "j" is exerted.

4. V(ij) = the "valence" that the focal person has for experiencing the "i"th outcome, given that effort level "j" is exerted.

(Note: the above assumes that there are "r" outcomes stemming from the successful attainment of this goal, wih "i" going from 1 to "r".)

Although models involving Vroom's valence, instrumentality and expectancy constructs have been used more often in survey research than research employing any other model of employee motivation, Vroom's theory has been properly tested in only a very few instances (Parker and Dyer, 1976). And even when the theory has been properly tested, the information that is yielded may not be the kind of information which management is looking for in the first place. An explanation of these issues is given below.

1.1 Vroom's Theory as a "Within-Persons" Model

The proper use of Vroom's theory should enable the researcher and management to determine what level of effort (e.g., low, medium or high) that a salesperson will be most likely to exert, based upon combinations of his valence, instrumentality and expectancy perceptions. However, this "effort" model of Vroom is usually (improperly) used to predict differences in performance levels between persons. In the latter application, one motivational force score is calculated for each individual as a combination of the valence, instrumentality and expectancy (VIE) constructs (whose magnitude does not vary at different effort levels), and this single "force" score is correlated with some external criterion variable, such as "sales" during the survey time period (Mitchell, 1974).

The researchers who have published empirically-based research on salesperson motivation and performance (Oliver, 1974; Churchill, Ford and Walker, 1976) have used a "between-persons" design in testing Vroom's theory. The model which Oliver (1974) used in his pioneer study concerning the prediction of salesperson motivation and performance computed the correlation of one "force" score with one "performance" score. The model that Churchill, Ford and Walker (1976) used in a later study is a "between-persons" model which incorporates multiple performance dimensions and involves the calculation of a "force" score for each performance dimension.

One may conjecture why most published research has used a "between-persons" operationalization of Vroom's theory. One possible reason is that sales management would like to gather information concerning the valence, instrumentality and expectancy constructs across members of the resident salesforce to make predictions relating to their effort and performance, and also to make generalizations across the salesforce with respect to these perceptions for diagnostic purposes and future use in sales personnel selection.

When Vroom's theory is (properly) implemented as a "within-persons" model, however, one generates predictions which relate to the idiosyncratic cognitions and affects of each salesperson. In this case, sales management is manifestly incapable of gathering information which would generalize across salespersons. The researcher, then, faces a dilemma when he wants to gather and analyze information on the VIE constructs across salespersons for the purpose of determining their motivation to perform on the job.

A model of salesperson motivation and performance which does allow one to measure and manipulate VIE constructs across subjects, and the one which closely approximates that used by Oliver (1974) and Churchill, Ford and Walker (1976), is one developed by Galbraith and Cummings (1967). In this study, the "expectancy" construct is essentially factored out of the calculation of motivational force scores. Galbraith and Cummings state that "expectancy" = E = 1.0, and qualitatively say that "expectancy" is the notion that "effort leads to performance". In their research design, a performance variable is regressed against seven instrumentality-valency combinations which relate to seven specific job outcomes.

Symbolically,

$$\text{Performance} = B(0) + B(1)\,(IV(1)) + \ldots + B(7)\,(IV(7)) + \text{error}$$

(Valence, "V", and Instrumentality, "I", are as defined previously.)

In spite of the fact that the "expectancy" measure used in this model does not make good intuitive or logical sense (Mitchell, 1974), the basic "between-persons" structure of the model does offer some promise for performing the motivational predictive and diagnostic functions across salespersons which management needs.

1.2 Measurement Issues in Research Using Vroom's Model

In his review article assessing the various strengths and weaknesses of Vroom's model and theory, Mitchell (1974) indicates that the "valence" construct which is used in his model has been shown to be redundant in a predictive sense when it is used as a "weight" for the "instrumentality" measure in empirical studies. The inference that one draws is that either Vroom's theory specifies incorrect relationships or that there are confounding VIE construct measurement issues which have not yet been uncovered.

Work done by Wilkie and Pessemier (1973) in the consumer attitudinal research literature offers a possible solution to this problem. This subject will be addressed at length in Chapter 3.

1.3 Intrinsic and Extrinsic Rewards (Outcomes) and Vroom's Theory

Though Vroom's model explicitly accommodates only externally mediated rewards (Vroom, 1964, p. 16), some authors (Porter and Lawler, 1968; Graen, 1969) have attempted to divide rewards or outcomes into intrinsic and extrinsic rewards, with the purpose of seeing which types of rewards are the best predictors of employee motivation and performance. It appears, however, that efforts to distinguish between variables on this basis (i.e., intrinsic outcomes vs. extrinsic outcomes) have not been successful (Dyer and Parker, 1975; Guzzo, 1979). The implication of the latter research is that, regardless of the perceived loci of mediation of job outcomes (rewards), outcomes cannot be successfully classified in any consistent manner as either intrinsic or extrinsic.

One possible reason that Porter and Lawler (1968) and Graen (1969) attempted to include intrinsic outcomes in a separate category is that they sensed the need to include variables which shed some light on the intrinsic nature of the jobs and how this might affect employee (salesperson, for instance) motivation. Recent research in organizational behavior (Steers and Spencer) shows that constructs are available which may be of assistance in achieving this end. This possibility is expanded upon in the next section.

1.4 Job Scope, Job Challenge and "Need Achievement"

As has been described previously, the conditional availability of job outcomes energizes behavior on the job in the framework of Vroom's theory. Furthermore, distinguishing between different kinds of outcomes in order to include variables in the model which relate to the intrinsic nature of the job as perceived by the salesperson is fruitless (Parker and Dyer, 1975; Guzzo, 1979). One avenue which appears to have promise in the development of a predictive model is one which incorporates job environment variables as well as job outcome variables. Job environment variables were first deemed to be important in work motivation in the human relations movement of the 1940's and 1950's. This movement offered the first major challenge to the Taylorian view of mankind's apparently predominant monetary motivation to work (McGregor, 1960). This movement held the tenets that:

1. It was incorrect to view all employees as lazy individuals who required constant close supervision and were motivated solely by money.

2. Workers are motivated to perform their jobs by factors other than money, such as the challenging nature of the job, satisfying interactions with co-workers.

Perhaps the most pervasive "prescription" to come out of this movement was the notion that jobs should be redesigned, or "enriched" in order to allow for greater employee challenge and a broader range of employee participation in the organization's activities. In short, the backers of the movement held that job environment issues were important in determining employee motivation.

1.5 Job Scope and Salesperson Motivation

To date, there has been no published research which empirically deals with the effects of an "enriched" job environment on the motivation and performance of salespersons. Pruden, Cunningham and English (1972) have reported on some relationships which exist between non-financial incentives and salesperson satisfaction. And Steers and Spencer (1977) indicate that "enriched" jobs—jobs with increased "scope"—increase motivation and performance levels of managers who are high in "need Achievement". Yet there is no such study which assesses the effects of what salespersons perceive to be an enriched job on their motivation and performance levels. Hackman and Oldham (1975) provide a questionnaire which allows the researcher to probe these aspects of job scope directly, thus allowing one the opportunity to determine whether a relationship exists, moderated or otherwise, between job scope and salesperson performance.

1.6 Participation, Job Challenge and "Need Achievement"

As business environments have become more complex and business operations more far-flung geographically, the implementation of formal management control systems has become more widespread. The use of these systems allows top management to direct, motivate and evaluate the actions of subordinate units of the company from a distance. The management control system which is, perhaps, the most widely heralded of any such system is the Management by Objectives (MBO) system.

1.6.1 Management by Objectives and Salesperson Performance

Management by Objectives, a management system which was popularized by Drucker (1954) and McGregor (1957), has been embraced by many corporations in the last two decades (Ivancevich, 1974). The fundamental steps of MBO are given below (Etzel and Ivancevich, 1974):

1. Meaningful operations objectives for the company are developed by top management.
2. Superiors and subordinates jointly participate in developing operations objectives for the subordinate units of the company, objectives which are consistent with the objectives developed by top management.

3. At the end of the evaluation period, superiors and subordinates jointly evaluate the subordinates' performance.

Advocates of MBO state that the strength of the system lies in the following sequence of psychological events which a subordinate supposedly experiences when he participates in the joint formulation of his objectives with his superior: participation in goal-setting leads to more involvement in the job, which, in turn, leads to greater commitment to fulfilling the goals and greater motivation and performance on the job (Futrell, Swan and Lamb, 1977; Jackson and Aldag, 1974). In short, greater participation by the subordinate is supposed to result in greater job performance by the subordinate.

There have been few empirical studies shedding light on the viability of the above sequence of events when applied in a sales environment. Ivancevich (1974) reported results supporting the viability of the MBO concept in describing a longitudinal study in which the effects of the institution of an MBO program in the marketing and production units of a company were investigated.

Other researchers, however, report mixed results with respect to salesperson motivation and performance when an MBO system is instituted by sales management (Futrell, Swan and Lamb, 1977). These authors indicate that the members of a salesforce which they studied did not experience the changes in perceptions of the management control system which would be predicted when an MBO system was instituted. In particular, they found the following to be the case:

1. The salesforce experienced a significant decrease (as opposed to the expected increase) in the perceived influence and control in the setting of performance goals and standards after the institution of the MBO system.

2. The members of the salesforce did not experience the expected significant increase in the clarity of goals when the management control system was thus changed.

3. The members of the salesforce did not perceive a stronger performance-rewards contingency relationship after the MBO system was installed.

Some perspective on these results can be found in an observation made by Etzel and Ivancevich (1974) in a survey article. In assessing the mixed results reported in a large number of empirical studies concerning the effectiveness of MBO as a management control system, the authors assert that the overall success of Management by Objectives cannot be ascertained directly because "what is viewed as MBO in one program would be considered autocratic, inflexible and non-participative in another organization".

By inference, one might expect the pattern of results reported by Futrell, Swan and Lamb to occur if sufficient organizational flexibility and subordinate participation already characterized the management control system prior to the institution of MBO. Under these circumstances, the MBO system might be viewed by the salesforce as being redundant, at best, and as a "whip" (Raia, 1964), at worst.

The above argument provides reasoning that the organizational context in which MBO is instituted affects the viability of the MBO program itself. From another point of view, Steers (1975) questions the appropriateness of any management program which emphasizes superior-subordinate participation in goal-setting, in general, and MBO, in particular. In doing this Steers shows that "need Achievement" moderates the relationship between superior-subordinate participation in goal-setting and subordinate performance on the job. Persons low in "n Ach" need the participation process in order to become ego-involved in achieving their goals, thus explaining the positive correlation between performance and participation for these persons. High "n Ach" individuals, however, view the process of participation as an unnecessary formality, the results of which may or may not be congruent with their own internally-set standards of performance. This reasoning would explain the lack of a significant correlation between participation in goal-setting for high "n Ach" persons and their job performance.

Steers would thus state that the use of a participation-based MBO system would be worthwhile for persons low in "need Achievement" and redundant for persons high in "n Ach". Scales developed by Steers (1976) can be used to determine whether the "need Achievement"-moderated relationship between participation and performance exists for salespersons as well. Light is thus shed as to the general (unmoderated) and well as specific (moderated) applicability of MBO as a management control system for the salesforce.

1.6.2 Job challenge

Job or task challenge is another task-goal attribute in Steers's inventory (1976) which represents a construct which has not been broached empirically in the sales management literature but which offers some potential as a predictor of salesperson motivation and performance. Job, or task, challenge has, however, received a significant degree of testing as a predictor of motivation and performance in experimental psychology and organizational behavior contexts. Yet, no consistency of results or unanimity of opinion exists as to the possible impact of this variable on salesperson motivation and performance. The specific predictions of the major motivational theories concerning how job challenge affects job performance are given below.

Locke (1978) theorizes that the more difficult the goals are that an individual has set for himself, the higher his performance will be. Steers (1975) modifies this stance in deducing from readings in research in "need Achievement" theory (Atkinson, 1958) that the challenge associated with difficult goals would probably serve as motivators mainly for persons high in "need Achievement". Persons low in "n Ach", he conjectured, would be repelled by the achievement-oriented challenge associated with having set difficult task or job goals. In reporting an attempt to empirically validate this notion, Steers could only provide results which appear to be in the predicted direction, but which are not statistically confirmable.

A closer reading of the works of Atkinson (1958) will enable one to specify a more precise relationship between "need Achievement" and job challenge than was presented in Steers's research. This more precise picture is given below.

John Atkinson (1958) has demonstrated in numerous laboratory experiments that an individual's perceived probability of suceeding at a given task—i.e., the challenge of the task—has a distinct motivating effect on the individual which in no way depends upon the nature of the reward (outcome) which the individual would receive for succeeding at the task. And, of relevance to the issue at hand, Atkinson indicates that the challenge of a task has different non-linear effects on persons with different "need Achievement" scores. For instance, a moderately challenging task (where the probability of succeeding at the task is about .5) will provide maximum positive motivation to perform for the person who is high in "n Ach", and high negative motivation for the person who is low in "need Achievement". On the other hand, having either a very challenging (prob. of success = .1) or a very easy (prob. of success = .9) task will provide the person low in "n Ach" with the least negative (avoidance) motivation. From a relative point of view, this situation is the most positive one for the person low in "n Ach" in terms of task challenge motivation.

1.6.3   A Comparison of Different Theories of Motivation

With the differing implications of the theories of Locke and Atkinson with respect to the relationship between perceived task challenge and performance in hand, one is afforded the opportunity to compare the predictions of the three main cognitive theories of motivation—those of Locke, Atkinson and Vroom. This comparison may be effected by transforming Locke's "goal difficulty" measure into a probabilistic measure of the respondent's chances of attaining his (her) sales production goal, and by performing a similar transformation on Vroom's expectancy (E) measure.

1.6.3.1   Predictions of Vroom's theory   In Vroom's theory and each variation of it, the expectancy measure (E) is based upon the "Law of Effect"—that is, the greater one's cognitively perceived chances of accomplishing something, the more likely that one is to attempt the act. In the context of Vroom's theory, one has the notion that the greater the expectancy is that one will achieve one's production goal, the greater is the Vroomian "force" measure and the greater the implied motivation for the person to attempt to achieve the sales production goal.

1.6.3.2 Predictions of Locke's goal-setting theory Locke, however, would state that the more difficult the production goal is, the greater the motivation to perform on the job to achieve this goal would be. Locke's theory states that

1. More specific goals are more motivating than less specific goals and,
2. More challenging goals are more motivating than less challenging goals.

As expectancy (E) goes down, Locke would say that motivation and performance would go up (contrary to the predicted effect of Vroom's expectancy notion).

1.6.3.3 Predictions of Atkinson's "need Achievement" theory Atkinson would state that for persons high in "n Ach", a moderately difficult production goal (E = .5) would be maximally stimulating (holding rewards constant). Very difficult (E = .1) or very easy (E = .9) goals would have the least positive motivational influence on the high "n Ach" salesperson. (The converse would be the case for low "n Ach" salespersons.)

A summary table of these predictions is given in Table 1.

Table 1. Motivation and Performance Predictions

Theory	Effects of an increase in expectancy (E) of "goal attainment" on motivation and performance	Relationship moderated by "n Ach"?
Vroom	monotonic INCREASE when expectancy (E) goes up	no
Locke	monotonic DECREASE when expectancy (E) goes up	no
Atkinson	non-monotonic, non-linear fluctuation when E goes up	yes

12   Introduction

1.7 A New Model for Predicting Salesperson Performance

In summary, it appears that constructs other than the job outcome variables focused upon in Vroom's model may prove to be useful in predicting the motivation and performance of salespersons. To this end, a basic conceptual model concerning the determinants of salesperson motivation and performance is proposed, the model which incorporates the findings of the research alluded to above. (Please see Figure 1 below.)

As it is depicted in Figure 1, the model considers:

1. Four independent variables
   a) Job scope (Steers and Spencer, 1977)
   b) Job challenge (Atkinson, 1958)
   c) Participation in goal-setting (Steers, 1976)
   d) Job outcomes (Oliver, 1974).
2. "need Achievement" (Murray, 1938), a moderator of the relationships between
   a) Job scope and job performance,
   b) Job challenge and job performance, and
   c) Participation in goal-setting and job performance.

Figure 1.   A Model for Predicting Salesperson Job Performance

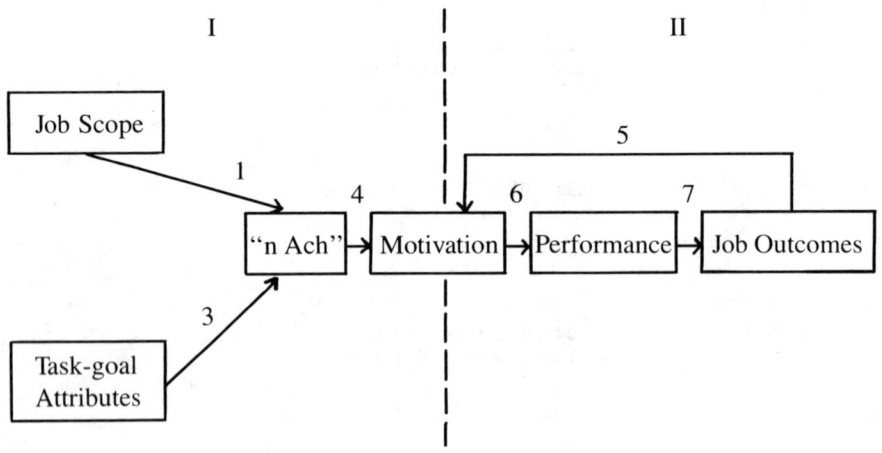

3. The dependent variable, job performance, which is multivariate in nature and is presumed to be directly related to motivational force (McClelland, et al., 1976).

In order to better understand how this model both incorporates the results of past research in salesperson motivation and performance and also summarizes potential relationships implied by research in other fields, please note the partitioning of the diagram into two parts, I and II, and the numbering of the projected casual relationships. The right hand portion of the diagram, designated by the roman numeral "II", represents the basic relationships uncovered by researchers using Vroom's model and variations thereof. These relationships are as follows.

In noting the conditional availability of job outcomes (signified by arrow (5)), the salesperson is motivated to perform on the job (arrow(6)) and presumably receives job outcomes for this performance (arrow(7)).

The relationships in the other half of the diagram, Partition I, are ones which are presumed to exist by assessment of the recent research findings and in no direct way call into question the basic truth of the relationships described in II. The relationships in I suggest that knowledge of issues other than the conditional availability of job outcomes may provide insight into additional significant determinants of salesperson motivation and performance.

Chapter 3 will develop in detail the operationalizations of the constructs in Figure 1 to be measured. However, to summarize these issues at this point, given below is a list of the research contributions of the proposed study.

Research Contributions

1. A "between-persons" VIE model for predicting salesperson motivation and performance similar to that used by Galbraith and Cummings, but one which has potential for overcoming the major problems which beset previous salesperson research using "between-persons" VIE-based models is given and tested.
   a) Refinements into the measurement of the VIE constructs which are indicated as viable by similar research in the consumer attitudinal research literature are given and the results described.
   b) The expectancy construct is defined precisely so as to avoid the logical fallacy encountered in assessing the corresponding construct in the model of Galbraith and Cummings.
2. Job scope and "task-goal attribute" variables as constructs which offer possible utility for increasing the concurrent performance prediction valid-

ities for the proposed model over that exhibited by research employing only Vroom's expectancy model or some variation thereof are described.

3. The predictive capabilities of the three main cognitive theories of motivation—those of Vroom, Atkinson and Locke—using a survey research design are compared.

4. The general viability of the application of "job enrichment" and "Management by Objectives" programs for sales management by conducting correlational studies relating job performance with job scope and "participation in goal-setting", respectively, is tested.

2

Literature Review

This chapter discusses the nature and development of the various theories of motivation to work in organizational environments. Particular emphasis is given to a comparison and contrast of the motivational predictions of these theories and how the model which this study proposes helps to reconcile the differences. Where relevant, insight is drawn from research by salesforce researchers, organizational behaviorists and experimental psychologists.

2.1 Nature of the Study of Motivation

The term "motivation" comes from the Latin verb, *movere* which means "to move". Ivancevich, et al., (1977) indicate that differing motivation theorists have developed differing viewpoints as to which concepts of motivation are emphasized in their research. These differing views come under three broad categories:

1. The analysis of motivation should concentrate on factors which arouse or incite a person's activities (Atkinson, 1964).
2. Motivation is a process-oriented term and is largely concerned with the study of human choice activities (Gibson, Ivancevich and Donnelly, 1976).
3. Motivation is concerned with how behavior is started, sustained or stopped. (Jones, 1955).

The theories of motivation which have received the most research attention in the past two decades fall under the first two categories listed above. Theories falling under the first category are known as "content" theories (Campbell, et al., 1970), since they are directed primarily toward isolating the factors which arouse a person to action. "Content" theories pay no overt attention to how these factors interact to produce the motivational force.

"Process" theories, on the other hand, focus upon describing how various factors interact to produce motivational force in humans. Most "process" theories relate to human choice behavior (Jacoby, 1976). Whereas, content theories describe which issues motivate a person, process theories relate how the issues interact to motivate the person.

An analogy concerning the relationship between content and process theories can be found in the relationship between primary and selective buying motives (Nicosia, 1966). Primary motives get one to arrive at the buying situation, and selective motives help one to choose among alternatives offered.

Campbell, et al, (1970) point out that while each of the two types of theories of motivation performs its own function, it would be desirable to develop a theory which performs the functions of both content and process theories simultaneously. No such model of motivation has been reported in the behavioral science literature to date. However, one of the purposes of this literature review is to both demonstrate that the elements for such a model can be found in recent research concerning human motivation, and to show how these elements might be combined to produce the model which this study presents.

2.2 Early Motivation Theories

Most theories of human motivation have been based upon the principle of "hedonism"—that principle which indicates that human beings act in such a fashion that they maximize their pleasure and minimize displeasure (Ivancevich, et al., (1977). The popularity of this concept dates back to the early Greek philosophers, with a revitalization coming from the writings of the English philosophers who were exponents of "Utilitarianism"—Locke, Mill and Bentham.

The notion that people are motivated to act according to the principle of hedonism proved to be too general in nature to prove (or disprove) when applied in an organizational setting. A more specific theory, proposed by F. W. Taylor (1911) at the turn of the century, was widely accepted for the first half of this century as the predominant theory of motivation of persons working in organizations. Taylor's approach to managerial motivation has been termed scientific management, for it addresses the study and design of work that would maximize worker efficiency.

The framework of Taylor's approach is based upon a number of premises concerning the individual worker. These premises center upon the notions that persons who work in organizations are naturally lazy and work only to receive money in compensation for services rendered.

2.2.1 Scientific Management and Salesperson Motivation

The notion that people are motivated to work solely by money has been firmly held by members of sales management as well as managerial in other areas of the organization. In one of the few empirical studies concerning salesperson motivation conducted prior to 1960, Haring and Myers (1953) concluded that salespeople were motivated to work mainly by money. Though this study was useful in that empirical data were gathered for analysis, the persons polled in the study were sales supervisors rather than salespersons, and there was no evidence of any validation of the results.

2.2.2 The Human Relations Movement in Management

The first major challenge to the "scientific management" view of persons working in organizations was the "human relations" movement, formally developed by Douglas McGregor (1960). McGregor asserted that workers were not naturally lazy and that they worked for a variety of reasons besides financial remuneration for services rendered. In particular, McGregor advocated:

1. Increased participation of workers in managerial decisions, and
2. The redesign or enrichment of workers' jobs to allow workers participation in a broader range of activities.

Prior to this study, there was no research looking into the effects of the "enrichment" of sales positions on the productivity of salespeople. In Chapter 4 are reported the results of tests assessing the effects of "job enrichment" on sales productivity of salespeople using a scale developed by Hackman and Oldham (1975).

2.3 The Major Formal Theories of Motivation

Though Taylor and McGregor were highly influential in bringing to light and clarifying issues which are central to the motivation of persons who work in organizations, their work can be best described as prescriptive in nature—that is, they developed assertions concerning the motivation of persons rather than theories concerning motivation which would be empirically testable. In order to trace the development of modern theories relating to the motivation of persons in organizations, one needs to assess the theories of motivation which laid the foundations for these modern theories.

According to Campbell and Pritchard (1976), each of the modern theories has its roots in one or more of the following theories: the theories of Skinner (1971), Hull (1952) and Lewin (1938).

2.3.1 Skinner's Reinforcement Theory

B. F. Skinner's "reinforcement theory" looks primarily at how motivated behavior is maintained over time. The three basic components of "operant conditioning"— the process which underlies reinforcement theory—are:

1. stimulus

2. response

3. consequences

A Skinnerian behaviorist might summarize the impact of reinforcement theory on organizational behavior as follows:

1. Some type of reinforcement is necessary to cause a change in behavior.

2. Some types of rewards are more effective than others in bringing about behavior change.

3. The speed and lasting nature of learning are determined by the timing of reinforcement (Ivancevich, et al., 1977).

As wide-ranging an impact as the theory has had on the community of experimental psychologists, this theory is excluded from further consideration in this study. The main reasons for doing this are summarized below:

1. Reinforcement theory has only been successfully validated on infrahuman subjects.

2. Reinforcement theorists have had major problems in arriving at operant definitions of some of the terms used in operant conditioning, such as "reinforcement" (Black, 1969).

2.3.2 The "Drive Theory" of Hull

Whereas, Skinner's "reinforcement theory" relied purely upon the stimulus-response-reinforcement paradigm of habit-formation to explain the motivation of subjects tested in the laboratory, C. L. Hull's "Drive" theory added two concepts to explain the motivation of the animals used in his research: the concepts of "drive" and "incentive". Using Hull's terminology, an individual's motivation or "reaction potential" for acting in a certain manner is a multiplicative function of:

1. The individual's past reinforcement history in similar situations;

2. the "drive" which the individual has to be incited to action, where "drive" represents a generalized kind of force to act which is independent of its source (e.g., hunger, fear, sex, etc.); and,

3. incentive, a "reward" if the subject performs in the proper fashion in the experiment.

Though Hull's theory is more inclusive than either Skinner's theory or Lewin's theory, "drive" theory suffers from the fact that researchers of this theory have been unable to prove with any adequate degree of validity that a generalized "drive" exists in human beings. Atkinson (1965) is credited with having "devastated" (Campbell and Pritchard, 1976) the notion that such an entity exists in human beings.

2.3.3 The Field Theory of Lewin

In contrast to the "hedonism of the past" orientation which the theories of Hull and Skinner have by virtue of their including "reinforcement" in their theories, the theory of Lewin is based upon "hedonism of the future". An explanation of this labelling accompanies the description of Lewin's theory below.

Lewin (1938) held that an individual's motivation to act in a given way is a function of the person's personality and the environment in which the person functions. Symbolically, one has:

$$\text{Motivation} = f(\text{personality}, \text{environment}).$$

The operationalization of this theory in an experimental setting centered upon the configuration of a person's "needs" (personality) and his "valences" for the "outcomes" (rewards) which stem from the successful negotiation of the experimental task (environment). The "hedonism of the future" label applies since the individual acts in such a way that he might in the future receive outcomes which he values. In contrast with Skinner's theory, Lewin's theory would assert that an individual could take an action which is directly counter to his reinforcement history if some new information led him to assign a higher "valence" to a given alternative of action than had been the case before.

Of special credit to the work of Lewin are the notions that (a) his theory was the first theory of motivation which was to be validated using human beings as subjects, and (b) his theory was the first theory of motivation to incorporate the idea that human beings are able to think and to develop "expectancies" and to make choices based upon "needs", "valences" and "expectancies". As such, Lewin (1938), together with Tolman (1932), is credited (Campbell and Pritchard, 1976) as having been instrumental in laying the foundations for the main cognitive theory of motivation used in organizational research settings today—the "expectancy" theory of Vroom (1964). Using the terminology presented previously, Vroom's theory is a "process" theory, and Vroom's theory and Adams's (1964) "equity" theory are described in the following section concerning "process" theories of motivation.

2.4 Process Theories of Motivation

The "process" theories of motivation which have received the most research attention in organizational settings in the past two decades are the theories of

Adams (1965) and Vroom (1964). A description of these theories and their possible utility for enabling the salesforce researcher to predict a salesperson's work motivation and performance is given below.

2.4.1 Equity Theory—J. S. Adams

Adams's equity theory is a cognitive theory of an individual's motivation to work in an organization. This theory is based upon the social comparison which the focal individual makes concerning the ratio of his own job "outcomes" to job "inputs" in comparison with the "outcome"/"input" ratio of a "reference person". Equity theory, which draws on Festinger's cognitive dissonance theory, states that the motivational level of an employee of an organization is determined by a three-step process:

1. The focal person compares his output/input ratio with the ratio of the reference person. (Here, "outputs" consist of such entities as pay, promotion and status, and "inputs" are entities such as effort, skills and education.)

2. The focal person makes a decision as to whether or not a state of "equity" exists, where his own ratio is equal to the perceived ratio of the reference person (who usually is a member of the focal person's organization).

3. If there is "equity", no further action; however, if "inequity" is perceived to exist, then the focal person will take action to help bring about equity.

The majority of research work done on equity theory has focused upon pay levels as the key "outcome" element of the ratio and effort as the primary "input" factor (Goodman and Friedman, 1971). The studies which have been conducted under these narrowly defined conditions (with pay as the main output and effort as the main input) have generated results which are largely in line with the predictions of equity theory. However, equity theory as it is currently viewed is unable to handle the inclusion of a broader range of inputs and outcomes. Also, some research indicates that individual differences may play a part in the determination on the part of the focal person as to what the relevant inputs should be. For example, some people view "responsibility" and "hard work" as something they must put into a job, thus excluding these variables from manipulation on the part of the focal person.

Little formal research concerning the application of equity theory in a salesforce environment has been published, though the results of a study done by Darmon (1974) may be interpreted in an equity theory context. Several researchers (Lawler, 1973; Campbell and Pritchard, 1976) have made arguments that Adams' equity theory can be subsumed under the general "umbrella" of the VIE model as an explanation and definition of the need for equity which, in turn, influences the valences for job outcomes. Attention is now turned to Vroom's (1964) "expectancy" theory of motivation.

2.4.2 The "Expectancy" Theory of Vroom

It is difficult to overestimate the importance of the work of Vroom (1964) to the field of motivation of persons working in organizations. More behavioral research concerning the motivation and performance of workers has been conducted using Vroom's theory than any other theory of motivation (Oliver, 1974). Vroom's (1964) theory states that the motivation to work at a given effort level is a function of:

1. The focal person's cognitive assessment (expectancy) as to the perceived probability that working at that effort level will lead to the person's achieving a work goal under consideration;
2. The affective assessment (valence) on the part of the focal person for the job outcomes (such as pay, promotion, recognition) which might stem from achieving the work goal considered in 1. above; and
3. The person's conative assessment (instrumentality) as to the causal relationship between achieving the work goal under consideration (in 1. above) and receiving the job outcomes (in 2. above).

(A more precise symbolic description of Vroom's theory is given in Chapter 1).

A variety of problems has accompanied the wide application of Vroom's model in experimental and survey settings. These problems can be classified under five categories, which are listed below:

1. Problems associated with the misspecification of Vroom's theory in research applications.
2. Empirical problems relating to properties assumed to be characteristic of the VIE constructs.
3. Problems with Vroom's theory as a model of cognitive choice processes in human thought.
4. Measurement problems associated with the VIE constructs.
5. Problems associated with the managerial application of Vroom's theory.

In the text which follows are elaborations on each of the problems which are listed above. After each of these elaborations is made, a description is given as to how the model of salesperson motivation which is presented in this study addresses the problem (when such a solution has been found in the literature).

2.4.2.1 Problems associated with theory misspecification Motivational research studies incorporating a misspecified version of Vroom's theory abound in the behavioral research literature (Mitchell, 1974). Problems arising from misspecification of Vroom's model usually occur when the researcher attempts to force Vroom's model to answer questions which Vroom's theory and model were never meant to answer (Campbell and Pritchard, 1976). Several instances of misspecification of Vroom's theory in salesperson motivational research are described below.

In the Churchill, Ford and Walker (1976) study, the model of salesperson motivation which was presented incorporated "performance" as a multivariate dependent variable, with each univariate member of the composite being continuous in nature. By contrast, the dependent variable in Vroom's model is univariate and discrete in nature, and "effort" is predicted, not "performance" (Mitchell, 1974).

Ivancevich, et al., (1977) point out the reasoning why "effort" and not "performance" should normally be the dependent variable in a test of Vroom's theory. Performance is affected by a variety of factors other than effort, such as:

1. Personality
2. Intelligence
3. Ability
4. The job itself
5. Supervisor's style
6. Reward system

This researcher would like to add other factors which specifically might affect the performance of a salesperson, such as the age of the salesperson, his tenure with the company, the sales potential of his territory and the span of control of the salesperson's supervisor.

It is not apparent that Oliver (1974) explicitly controlled for any of these factors in his choosing to explain salesperson "performance" rather than salesperson "effort" on the job. Churchill, Ford and Walker (1976) do include salesperson ability and role perceptions as parts of their model, though empirical results reflecting on the validity of their model have not been reported in the literature.

The model proposed in this study does explicitly control for personality ("need Achievement") and job ("job design" and "task-goal attribute") factors. In addition, the last four factors given which present bias specific to sales positions are controlled for through the use of a procedure given by Ryans and Weinberg (1978), which is explained in detail in Chapter 3.

The model proposed in this study excludes measures of a salesperson's ability and intelligence as being valid explanatory factors of sales performance. Ghiselli (1973) reports that efforts to use measures of "ability" or "intelligence" to explain sales performance have been unsuccessful.

Also, attempts to relate "reward system" to "motivation" have generally been unsuccessful. Work by Deci (1975) reflects on how the nature of the reward system administered by a company may affect the nature of the motivation of the salesperson on the job. Though Deci presents evidence which suggests that conditionally available rewards (such as a direct commission on sales) should decrease intrinsic motivation and increase extrinsic motivation in salespeople, Calder and Staw (1975) have given counter reasoning which better explains Deci's results. Thus, the model proposed in this study does not include "reward system" as a predictor variable.

Except for "supervisor's style", the model presented in this study accounts for all of the factors in the list of Ivancevich, et al., (1977) which have been validly shown to have a systematic effect on "performance". Thus, this researcher feels justified in using "performance" rather than "effort" as the dependent variable in the model of salesperson motivation presented in this study.

A related problem in the Churchill, Ford and Walker (1976) study stems from the notion that the authors operationalize Vroom's model as a "between-persons" model, where each of several performance scores is correlated with a motivational "force" score, and an overall correlation for the entire sample is made for each performance dimension. In Vroom's theory, however, a separate and unique prediction as to what level of effort will be expended is made for each member of the sample, thus bearing out the reasoning for describing Vroom's model as a "within person" model.

The survey design used by Oliver (1974) can also be characterized as a "between-persons" design, since correlations for the overall sample were generated. The main problem here is one of "misrepresentation". Though statements are made to the contrary (Oliver, 1974; Churchill, Ford and Walker, 1976), the above researchers are not using Vroom's model. They are using a model which is one in a class of many expectancy-instrumentality-valence models. Perhaps, their model is closer kin to the model of Porter and Lawler (1968) than the model of Vroom (1964).

The portion of the model proposed in Part II of Figure 1 in this study is closer kin to the model of Cummings and Galbraith (1967) than to the model of Vroom. Thus, this model cannot be validly criticized on the grounds that it presents a misrepresentation of Vroom's model as a "between-persons" model.

The conceptualization of the "expectancy" construct has been especially troublesome for motivation researchers (Mitchell, 1974). For instance, in one application (Cummings and Galbraith, 1967), "expectancy" is defined as the notion that "effort leads to performance". Defined as such, "expectancy" is always equal to 1.0 and is, effectively, factored out of the research design as being a useful variable.

In the proposed model, the "expectancy" term is defined very precisely and should conform to the demands placed upon it by rigorous experimental research (Atkinson, 1964). Chapter 3 goes into this issue in detail.

Misconceptualization of the "expectancy" variable is not the only problem which has been associated with this construct. When Vroom's VIE model has been used in motivational research, the expectancy variable has not been shown to vary empirically in the fashion which Vroom's theory posits. This concern is discussed in the next category of problems occurring in research using Vroom's model and theory.

2.4.2.2 Empirical problems related to the VIE constructs There are two properties of the constructs of Vroom's model which are assumed to hold true. These properties are listed and expanded upon below.

(1) The expectancy variable should fluctuate according to the "Law of Effect"—that is, the greater the expectation that a task can be successfully accomplished, the greater the motivation is to attempt to accomplish that task.

The "Law of Effect" implies that a positive monotonic relationship exists between expectancy and motivation. However, experimental laboratory work done by Atkinson (1964) indicates that the component of motivation produced by the expectancy variable varies according to a quadratic, non-linear formulation. Other work done by Locke, et al., (1970) indicates that there is a negative relationship between expectancy and motivation. Thus, the case is by no means settled that the "Law of Effect" unequivocally defines the relationship between expectancy and motivation.

(2) The expectancy, valence and instrumentality constructs need to be independent of each other.

Vroom's theory requires that expectancy, valence and instrumentality variables function independently of each other. However, in the great majority of studies purporting to use Vroom's model, this has not been shown to be the case (Mitchell, 1974). In particular, "valence" and "instrumentality" are typically positively correlated.

Currently, no methodology exists to account for or remove this correlation. Thus, in Part II of the model presented in Figure 1 of this study, there are positive correlations among the constructs, especially between the "instrumentality" and "valence" variables. This correlation is related to the third category of problems characterizing VIE-based research.

2.4.2.3 The model of Vroom as representing valid thought processes The consistent and significant positive relationships between valence and instrumentality which have been uncovered in the great majority of VIE-based studies lead one to believe that these two entities may not be clearly distinguishable in human thought. If these constructs are, indeed, related in human cognitive processes, then Vroom's model does not hold.

A related problem is that "research evidence does not support the notion that individuals mentally perform the complex multiplicative calculations required by the model before effort is exerted". (Ivancevich, et al., 1977). If this is true, then positive correlations found in Vroomian-based model studies might need to be classified as merely suggesting conditionally valid relationships until further evidence is produced which favors the Vroom formulation. The $\Sigma(I\ V)$ configuration which is used in Part II of the proposed model in Figure 1 is not being used because this formulation has received unassailable empirical validation as representing a viable human thought process but because it is the best such representation known of in the research concerning human motivation today.

2.4.2.4 Variable measurement problems (a) An issue related to the above concern centers upon variable measurement problems which may occur when one multiplies the constructs in the fashion indicated in Vroom's model (simply stated, $F = E(\Sigma I\ V)$. Schmidt (1973) demonstrates that the VIE constructs need to be measured on a ratio scale (an interval scale with a rational zero point) before the correlation of sums of cross products can be generated in a mathematically valid fashion. If the scales do not have this property, Schmidt shows that the sums of cross products generated by the VIE operations may fluctuate drastically when transformations are applied which would be invariant if the scales possessed ratio properties.

The issue here, then, is that to the extent that the VIE scales used fail to demonstrate ratio properties, the products of the mathematical operations performed will fail to be valid. Again, no technology or methodology has been presented in the literature which enables the researcher to overcome this problem in this situation, so mention will be made of this issue as a possible qualifier of the results generated in this study. A technique known as "conjoint analysis" is currently being tested to see if its application can enable the researcher to transform the scales used in VIE research to ratio scale, thus overcoming this measurement problem.

(b) Another measurement problem concerns the construct validity of the dependent variable, "effort", in Vroom's model. Williams and Seiler (1973) demonstrate that measures of "effort" have low discriminant and convergent validity. "Performance" variables, on the other hand, were shown to possess adequate validities in these areas. Since job "performance" has been used in this study, then the construct validity of the dependent variable used is less of a problem than would be the case if Vroom's model were strictly adhered to.

26 Literature Review

(c) The final measurement problem addressed concerns the low correlations between the dependent variable and the independent variables used in Oliver's (1974) study being attributable to what Oliver calls "heterogeneity of respondents". Though Oliver did not precisely specify what he meant by this term, a similar kind of situation has been reported in studies concerning linear attitudinal research models (Churchill, 1972; Sheth and Talarzyk, 1972; Wilkie and Pessemier, 1973). Linear models used in attitudinal research have a form that is precisely analogous to the VIE model used in motivation research.

In the attitudinal research literature, "heterogeneity of respondents" would correspond to the phenomenon whereby each individual subject demonstrates a unique variance in answering items used to measure attitudinal constructs. Bass and Wilkie (1973) state very succinctly the problem which occurs when individuals exhibit differing response "dispersions" in assigning scores to attitudinal construct:

> "Unweighted variables summed into a composite weight themselves in proportion to their standard deviations."

In neither of the two empirical studies which concern salesperson motivation and which employ a (variation of) Vroom's model has this issue been broached in any form. A solution to this problem would appear to lie in dividing the score on the "instrumentality" and "valence" items of each respondent by the standard deviations exhibited by the respondent in answering items in each of these areas, respectively.

2.4.2.5 Managerial application problems The last type of problem characterizing research using a Vroomian model comes not from any inherent difficulty with applying the theory in a situation where it was originally intended to be used—as a "within person" behavioral choice model making predictions concerning which one of several discrete effort levels at which a worker would perform. "Managerial application" problems stem from the fact that the model does not account for other issues which have been shown to have motivational implications for persons working in organizations. Some of these other issues may refer to the "design" of a job (Steers and Spencer, 1977) and the "task-goal characteristics" of the job (Steers, 1975). (These issues are dealt with at length in the next section, concerning "content" theories of motivation.

Also, members of sales management need a model of motivation which will allow them to gather information across salespersons and to possibly make generalizations concerning, for instance, (a) the specific kinds of (second level) job outcomes that high performing salespersons prefer, and (b) how the "valence for performance" (defined in this study as the sum of the instrumentalities for the five most important job outcomes, weighted by the valences for each of these second level job outcomes) can be defined and related to job performance. To this end, this researcher is using a framework presented by Galbraith and Cummings (1967).

As has been noted before, there is a problem with the definition with the "expectancy" variable used in Galbraith and Cummings. In Chapter 3 a new focus for the "expectancy" variable will be given and will show not only why this new operationalization appears to have superior characteristics to other definitions of "expectancy" reported in the literature, but also will demonstrate how an empirical assessment of fluctuations in this new "expectancy" variable have allowed the researcher to give confirmation to the validity of one of the three major cognitive theories of motivation (Atkinson, 1964; Locke, 1970; and Vroom, 1964).

2.4.3 Results of Formal Extensions of Vroom's Model

A final comment on problems related to Vroom's model relates to the success of models which are ostensibly formal extensions of Vroom's model. Porter and Lawler (1968) and Graen (1969) describe models which are elaborations on Vroom's (1964) theory and model. In their models, improved effort and/or performance predictions are sought by making the distinction between "intrinsic" and "extrinsic" outcomes, with the loci of mediation of these outcomes being internal to the individual, and external to the individual, respectively. Dyer and Parker (1975) and Guzzo (1979) give convincing arguments that such a distinction cannot be validly made on any existing level of analysis. Under these circumstances, the models which Porter and Lawler (1968) and Graen (1969) present necessarily collapse back into the original formulation of Vroom (1964), which makes no overt distinction between different kinds of outcomes.

2.4.4 Vroom's Model vs. Part II of the Research Model

Apparently, Part II of the model proposed in Figure 1 in Chapter 1 differs from Vroom's model and theory. Rather than representing a refutation of Vroom's theory, Part II of the proposed model in Figure 1 addresses different questions, ones related to the effects of a salesperson's valences for second level outcomes on his job motivation. Whereas, Vroom's model looks at which of several effort levels that a salesperson might be motivated to perform at on the job, the model in Figure 1 draws upon the preponderance of evidence which suggests that a person's "valence for (second level) job outcomes" is positively related to the person's motivation and performance on the job, irrespective of the impact which the person's perceived "expectancy" of attaining a job-related goal has on the person's motivation (Campbell and Pritchard, 1976).

In the model given in Figure 1, "expectancy" is treated as an entity which is logically separate in its motivational implications from the "valence for performance" entity, which is the subject of Part II of Figure 1. Expectancy is treated as a "task-goal attribute", in the words of Steers (1976). This placement of expectancy in Part I of Figure 1 is due to the existence of much research (Atkinson, 1964; Locke, et al., 1970) which suggests that this construct does not fluctuate according to the "Law of Effect", which underlies Vroom's (1964) formulation.

As entities distinct from the valence and instrumentality variables, the constructs in Part I of Figure 1 are reported to have motivational implications for members of management (Steers and Spencer, 1977; Steers, 1975; Atkinson, 1964). Determining whether or not these variables have similar implications for the members of the salesforce is one of the purposes of this study. These constructs have not been found to be part of any clearly defined cognitive choice processes; thus, research concerning these constructs could be classified under the "content" category of motivation theories. "Content" theories of motivation constitute the second major category of theories of motivation, and the main theories falling in this category are described below.

2.5 Content Theories of Motivation

Whereas, "process" theories of motivation such as the theories of Vroom and Adams are more oriented toward making predictions concerning the extent of an individual's motivation based upon explicit and rational choice processes, "content" theories of motivation place greater emphasis on what it is that arouses motivation in the individual. There are three theories of motivation which have received much attention in research circles and acclaim in managerial circles. These are the theories of Herzberg (1959), Maslow (1954) and Alderfer (1972).

2.5.1 *The Theory of Herzberg—"Satisfiers" and "Dissatisfiers"*

In an extensive study using the critical incident methodology of response elicitation, Herzberg (1959) asked the accountants and engineers of a firm to describe what the circumstances were of their (1) moments of greatest happiness, and (2) moments of greatest unhappiness while working for the firm. An assessment of the responses indicated that the moments of greatest happiness usually concerned the content of the respondent's functioning in the job itself, such as high accomplishment and praise for good job performance. The times of greatest displeasure usually concerned contextual matters, such as pay problems. It appeared to Herzberg that contextual problems—or "dissatisfiers", in the words of Herzberg—were related to the content-oriented "satisfiers" in that the existence of a significant number of "dissatisfiers" on the job would preclude the positive, accomplishment-oriented "satisfiers" from motivating the employee to work.

Though the intuitive appeal of Herzberg's theory is strong, there are two problems associated with the study which appear to inhibit further research into the theory:

1. The division of the factors into satisfiers and dissatisfiers oversimplifies the nature of job satisfaction; and
2. Factors which function as satisfiers for one person may function as dissatisfiers for another person, depending upon the age of the person and other personal characteristics (Whitsett and Winslow, 1967).

The notion suggested in 2. above that different entities can be more (or less) motivating to a person at, say, different times in a person's life is one of the implications of the next "content" theory of motivation, based upon Maslow's "Need Hierarchy".

2.5.2 The "Need Hierarchy" of Motivation—Maslow

Perhaps the theory of motivation most widely heralded in managerial circles focuses upon Maslow's (1954) "Need Hierarchy". Maslow's theory is based upon three fundamental assumptions:

1. A person's needs are arranged in a hierarchy of importance, starting with (a) self-actualization, and going down through (b) ego, status and esteem, (c) social, (d) safety and security, and ending with (e) physiological needs.
2. Only unsatisfied needs can influence behavior.
3. When a person's needs at a lower level in the hierarchy are minimally satisfied, the person can be motivated only by needs at higher levels in the hierarchy.

The theory is clear, intuitively appealing and easy for the layman to remember. However, the theory has received very little empirical support. Hall and Nougaim (1968) reported results which were disconfirming for Maslow's theory in a thorough longitudinal study done using members of A. T. & T's Management Progress Study. In the salesforce research area, Churchill, Ford and Walker (1976) reported mixed results in their attempt to demonstrate that a salesperson's "valence" for job-related rewards follows Maslow's hierarchy as the salesman aged and gained tenure with the company.

A theory which appears to better explain the results of many studies testing the validity of Maslow's hierarchy has been developed by Alderfer (1972). The tenets of this theory are elaborated upon in the next section.

2.5.3 The ERG Theory of Alderfer

The final "content" theory to be assessed, Alderfer's ERG theory, represents a variation on Maslow's Need Hierarchy. Instead of the five level hierarchy described above, Alderfer's hierarchy has three levels: existence, relatedness and growth (or ERG, in short). Unlike Maslow's model the hierarchy in Alderfer's model is not "strict" in that the needs of persons fluctuate up and down among the three levels according to the three rules given below:

1. The less each level of need has been satisfied, the more it will be desired.
2. The more lower level needs are satisfied, the greater is the desire for the higher level needs.
3. The less higher level needs are satisfied, the more lower level needs will be desired.

A key distinction between Maslow's Need Hierarchy and Alderfer's ERG model is that Maslow's hierarchy is just need satisfaction-progressive—that is, one only travels up the hierarchy. Under Alderfer's scenario, one may both go up his hierarchy (satisfaction-progressive) and go down the ERG hierarchy (frustration-regressive). According to Ivancevich, et al., (1977), many behavioral researchers view ERG theory as "the most current, valid and researchable theory of motivation based upon 'need'".

2.5.4 An Assessment of the Predictive Utility of "Need" Theories

One major drawback of the three "content" theories described above in helping one to predict salesperson motivation and performance is that they primarily predict what motivates a person rather than to what extent the person is motivated—the latter which is of great importance in making such predictions. What is desirable, then, is to develop a theory of motivation and an accompanying model which both performs the function of "content" models of motivation by giving a specification of as many different kinds of entities which motivate salespeople to perform on the job and, at the same time, describe how much these entities motivate the person—thus performing the function of the "process" theory. The theory of Lewin (1938), which has been previously described, appears to present just such a framework. According to Campbell and Pritchard (1976), "Lewin viewed the force on an individual to be combination of the push of need tensions and the pull of highly valent outcomes." Thus, his theory sets the framework for a model which both accomplishes the task of specifying what motivates salespersons (e.g., needs and valences) and the extent to which they are motivated by these entities. The model presented in Figure 1 represents an ostensive attempt to impute motivational importance to "need" and "valence" constructs simultaneously and to allow for the possibility of measuring their relative importance in motivating salespeople to perform on the job.

Works in experimental psychology and organizational behavior have helped to define the structure of Part I, especially, in Figure 1 (Atkinson, 1964; Steers and

Spencer, 1977; and Steers, 1975). A description of this work and how these studies have been instrumental in formulating the proposed model is given below.

2.6 Atkinson, Steers and Locke

The works of Atkinson, Steers and Locke have been instrumental in helping this researcher to formulate the model presented in this research. Atkinson has presented convincing evidence that the "expectancy" construct does not function according to the fashion dictated by Vroom's theory and that the "need Achievement" construct helps to determine the precise impact that "expectancy" will have on motivation. Steers showed that knowledge of a person's need to achieve will affect his motivational receptivity to "job enrichment" and Management by Objectives (MBO) programs. Finally, Locke was instrumental in showing how goals mediate the effects of a person's valence for job outcomes on the person's motivation. The works of each of these authors is discussed, in turn below.

2.6.1 The "need Achievement" Theory of Motivation—Atkinson

John Atkinson's "need Achievement" theory of motivation is, perhaps, the most rigorously researched cognitive theory of motivation of all such theories to be developed in the experimental laboratory (DeCharms, 1978). His theory states that a person's motivation to perform an act is primarily a function of four variables:

1. The person's motive to succeed, as measured by the "need Achievement" construct.
2. The person's perceived probability of successfully accomplishing the act under consideration.
3. The person's incentive to succeed.
4. Extrinsic motivation.

Symbolically, one has:

Motivation = (Motive × Pr(Success) × Incentive) + extrinsic motivation

or,

Motivation = (Motive × Pr(Success) × (1 − Pr(Suc.))) + extr. motiv.

There are several points concerning the above formulation which are of interest:

1. The person's "incentive" to succeed at a task under consideration is given

as a cognitive entity and is equal to $(1 - \Pr(\text{Suc.}))$: the lower the perceived probability of successfully accomplishing the task, the greater the incentive to succeed, and vice versa.

2. The "Achievement motivation" which is elicited when Pr(Success) ranges from 0 to 1.0 varies quadratically and is at a maximum when the probability of success $= .5$.

3. According to Atkinson, "Achievement Motivation" has a positive motivating effect on persons who are high in "need Achievement" and a negative motivating effect on persons who are low in "need Achievement". Thus, where the probability of achieving an act (such as "making sales quota") is equal to approximately .5, the person high in "n Ach" has the greatest positive achievement motivation to perform, and the person low in "n Ach" has the greatest negative achievement motivation to perform. The only thing which induces the person low in the need for achievement to perform on the job is the existence of "extrinsic motivation".

Though Atkinson's theory has been classified by Campbell and Pritchard (1976) as a "process" theory of motivation, it can also be classified as a "content" theory by virtue of the fact that the definition and interaction of sources of "extrinsic motivation" are not made explicit. Though Atkinson's hybrid content/process theory accommodates fluctuations in the four variables listed above, another issue less central to Atkinson's work is particularly relevant to the model presented in this study. This is the notion that job characteristics intrinsic to the degree of enrichment of the job positively motivate persons high in "n Ach" on the job, and leave unaffected or negatively motivate persons low in "need Achievement". Work done by Steers and Spencer (1977) validates this relationship. This work is described in the next section.

2.6.2 Research Done by Richard Steers

Work done by Steers (Steers and Spencer (1977); Steers (1975); and Steers (1976)) has not been done ostensibly to develop a new theory of motivation of persons working in organizations but represents an affirmation of the important role which the "need Achievement" construct—as developed by Murray (1938) and implemented by Atkinson (1964)—plays in work motivation. In particular, knowledge of a manager's need for achievement has been shown to be instrumental in determining the degree and nature of his motivational receptivity to (a) job enrichment and (b) MBO programs.

2.6.2.1 Job design and work motivation The notion that aspects intrinsic to the nature or design of a job may have motivational implications is not new to research in experimental psychology and organizational behavior. Attempts on the part of Porter and Lawler (1968) and others to make the distinction between "extrinsic" and "intrinsic" job outcomes and to imply the existence of differing loci of mediation (external and internal to the individual, respectively) for these outcomes appears to be a product of this sentiment. Also, as was stated previously, Atkinson (1964) reports that whereas persons high in "n Ach" are positively motivated by the intrinsically motivating aspects of a job, persons low in "n Ach" are "demotivated" by these aspects intrinsic to the nature of the job.

The "need Achievement" construct served as the basis for work done by Steers and Spencer (1977), which reported the relationship between "job design" and "job performance" for managers. In this study, empirical results bore out the notion posited by Atkinson (1958) that persons high in "n Ach" are positively motivated to perform by their perceptions of the "enrichment" of the job. One of the objectives of this study is to report on the relationship between "job design" (or job enrichment) and the sales performance of salespeople. The scale used to test this notion was developed by Hackman and Oldham (1975), and is an improved version of the scale used by Steers and Spencer (1977).

2.6.2.2 Task-Goal attributes and work motivation In other work by Steers (1975) the effects of the "task-goal attributes" on work motivation are investigated. "Task-goal attributes" are those attributes which underlie Management by Objectives (MBO) programs and refer to such issues as (1) the clarity of the task at hand (such as "making quota"), (2) the quantity of feedback received from the supervisor, and (3) the degree of participation between worker and supervisor in deciding upon what the worker's goal should be.

One area of research which is particularly pertinent to the effects of "task goal attributes" on job performance is the work of Locke (Locke, Cartledge and Knerr, 1970; Locke, 1978) concerning the "goal-setting" process. Locke's goal-setting theory is not a theory of motivation, per se, but is a theory which outlines how goals mediate and govern the effects of valent job outcomes on effort and performance. Underlying Locke's theory are four statements describing how different aspects of goals and the goal-setting process affect job performance.

1. The more specific goals are, the greater will be the job performance which is forthcoming.

2. The more frequent the feedback given to the worker, the more motivated to perform the worker will be.

3. The more difficult a goal is, the greater will be the performance, as long as the worker is committed to the goal.

4. The more participation that takes place in making the goal, the better will be the forthcoming performance.

Campbell and Pritchard (1976) make explicit properties of Locke's theory which are complementary to Vroom's "expectancy" theory:

1. Goals or intentions give behavior direction. They are thus non-motivational in nature in that they reflect what is to be done rather than reflecting which entities are more attractive.
2. Changes in a person's "valence" for job outcomes can change behavior only insofar as a change in Valence is coupled with a change in goals.
3. An individual is satisfied (or dissatisfied) with goals only insofar as actual performance matches the individual's goals.

Though Latham and Yukl (1975) report fairly wide empirical confirmation of the effects of the goal-setting process on job performance, Locke's framework does not account for the effects of individual differences on the goal-setting/job performance relationship. The work of Steers (1975) does allow for the effects of individual differences on job performance as mediated by the "task-goal attributes".

Steers (1975) found that a "need Achievement"-moderated relationship exists between a person's perceptions of "task-goal attributes" and his job performance. In particular, he found that:

1. having specific individual goals was functional in increasing the job performance of persons high in "need Achievement", and not necessarily functional for persons low in the need to achieve;
2. the job performance of persons low in "n Ach" is increased by "participation in goal-setting", but is left unchanged for persons low in the need to achieve;
3. persons high in "n Ach" respond positively to receiving frequent feedback, with no such relationship existing for their low "n Ach" counterparts.

In Chapter 4 of this study, the results are given which report the relationships between "task-goal attributes" and the job performance of the salespeople in the sample.

2.7 Conclusion

All of the components of the model given in Figure 1 have now been explained in detail. Chapter 3 gives the precise operationalization of these components in the questionnaire used, and Chapter 4 gives the results of the empirical investigations and analyses.

3

Research Methods

This chapter reviews the research methods used in this study. The sample data gathering techniques, constructs measured and the corresponding scales employed, and data analysis procedures to be used will be discussed in depth. Particular emphasis is given to a description of the rationale for using a new definition of the "expectancy" variable. Also, the description of a new salesperson "performance" variable which is statistically corrected for sources of bias caused by "managerially controllable and external, non-psychological variables" is given.

3.1 Sampling Procedure

Many of the previous empirical studies examining the relationship between salesperson performance and motivation have used the members of the salesforce of one or two companies as the sample frame (Oliver, 1974; Churchill, Ford and Walker, 1976). As a result, the findings which were reported might be classified as company-specific in nature. In order to provide a sample frame which will allow the researcher to make more generalized statements concerning the motivational determinants of salespeople's behavior on the job, empirical data from the members of the salesforces of three different companies were gathered and analyzed. These companies were drawn from the textile industry, the transportation industry and the industrial metal wrapper manufacturing industry. Access to management of the textile company was gained through introductions generated by a Professor of Textiles at N. C. State University. The head of Corporate Development for the University of North Carolina School of Business Administration was instrumental in introducing this researcher to sales management of the transportation company and of the industrial metal wrapper manufacturer.

It was felt that in choosing firms from different industries, one would gain information concerning the perceptions of job activities of salespersons who function in a broad class of selling situations. By selecting the sample frame in this fashion, the researcher hoped to avoid having to classify the results which stem from this research as "firm specific".

3.2 Data Collection Procedure

The data gathering instruments were self-administered questionnaires. The questionnaires were mailed by management of participating firms to the members of their respective salesforces. Both the salespersons and the sales managers completed the questionnaires and returned them in pre-addressed and stamped envelopes. Table 2 gives a summary of:

1. The focal variables and constructs measured.
2. The types of individuals who responded to the above variables and constructs.

In order to formally introduce the project to the salespersons and their first-line sales managers, a notification letter was sent by the Vice-President of Sales to each participating salesperson and sales manager. This letter stated that the company was participating in a study concerning salesperson motivation and performance and that each salesperson and sales manager is strongly encouraged to participate. This notification letter emphasized the confidentiality of each individual's response and encouraged the respondent to answer each item in the questionaire as frankly as is possible. (See Appendix.) An additional letter was sent to each salesperson and sales manager from this researcher and gave a summary briefing as to the purpose of the study. (See Appendix.)

Accompanying the questionaire—which was sent approximately two weeks after the above "notification" letters were mailed—are two cover letters, given in the Appendix, pp. 117 and 118. The first is the draft of the cover letter from the Vice-President of Sales to each salesperson and sales manager. The second is the draft of the cover letter from the researcher to each salesperson and sales manager. These cover letters provided further reinforcement as to the confidentiality of the respondents' answers and further clarified the nature of the study and the benefits which will be afforded the members of the salesforce and sales management as a result of the salespersons' and sales managers' participation in the project.

In the questionnaire, information was obtained from three sales organizational members concerning the focal salesperson. The response rates for the three companies used are given in Table 3.

The salesperson supplied information concerning the following variables.

1. The valence, expectancy and instrumentality variables relevant to Vroom's (1964) and Galbraith and Cummings' (1967) models of motivation.
2. Job scope variables (Hackman and Oldham, 1975).

Table 2. Research Design

Proposed Psychological Factors Affecting Salesperson Performance	Questionnaire Respondent
Task environment --Job scope	Salesperson

Task-goal attributes
  --Job Challenge
  --Participation in Goal-setting
	Salesperson

Salesperson Individual Diffs. --"need Achievement"	Salesperson
Job Outcomes	Salesperson
Proposed Non-Psychological Factors affecting Salesperson Performance	
Sales Mgr. Span of Control	Salesperson
Sales Territory Potential	Salesperson
Sales Territory Geographic Dispersion	Salesperson
Sales Experience	Salesperson
Performance Measures to be Used	
"Sales--Statistically Adjusted for Biassing elements	Salesperson and Sales Manager
A Subjective Measure of Sales Performance	Sales Manager
"Sales" - unadjusted	Sales Manager
An Objective measure relative to Quota	Sales Manager

3. Murray's "need" constructs (Steers and Braunstein, 1976).
4. Steers's task-goal attributes (Steers, 1976).
5. Jackson Preference Scale for "need Achievement" (Jackson, 1967).
6. Biographical Data.

Table 3. Company Participation

COMPANY	NUMBER OF SALESMEN			NUMBER OF SALES MANAGERS		
	SURVEYED	PART	%	SURVEYED	PART	%
COMPANY I	77	47	61	14	14	100
COMPANY II	150	31	21	40	27	68
COMPANY III	13	11	85	1	1	100
TOTALS	240	89	37	55	42	76

Also, sales managers supplied information concerning the job performance of the focal salesperson in the fiscal year just prior to the gathering of information. (The issue of performance measurement is a major topic and is given intensive coverage later in this chapter.)

3.3 Hypotheses to be Tested

The information to be gathered in the study was instrumental in testing the concurrent validity of the following hypotheses alluded to in Chapter 1.

1. Contingently available job outcomes motivate a salesperson to expend effort in a sales environment. (Denoted by (5)-(6)-(7) in Figure 1.)

2. "Need Achievement" moderates the job scope-job performance relationship for salespersons (signified by the (1)-(4)-(6) relationship in Figure 1).

3. "Need Achievement" moderates the relationship between "participation in goal-setting" and job performance. (Signified by the (3)-(4)-(6) relationship in Figure 1.)

4. When "expectancy" is defined as the perceived probability that the salesperson will achieve his own personal goals, "need Achievement" moderates the relationship between "expectancy" and sales performance.

It is important to note that the concurrent (rather than predictive) validity of the above hypotheses was tested. The salespersons and sales managers were asked to use the performance data for the past fiscal year as the proper perspective. Also, when the focal salesperson was asked to supply information concerning his own personal psychological make-up (e.g., "n Ach") and other subjectively assessed variables (e.g., "Job Scope"), this salesperson was asked to give his (her) answer based on the perspective of the past year, 1979.

One might conjecture that this kind of procedure would not allow the researcher to detect changes in the constructs to be measured which took place throughout the fiscal year under assessment (in which the salesperson participated in selling activity). Maslow's (1954) theory, one might argue, states that a salesperson's "higher order needs" would take on greater significance as his "lower order needs" become satisfied.

There is growing evidence that an individual's "needs" and "valences" do not change over time and do not even change when important events such as job "promotion" take place in the individual's life. Lawler and Suttle (1972) show as fallacious Maslow's "prepotency" notion that "higher order" needs permanently supplant the "lower order" needs when the "lower order" needs are satisfied. Festinger (1964) indicates that "motive" and "value" orientations seem to be unchanged by promotion. Also, Gilbert Churchill, Jr., states in a forthcoming article (personal conversation with this researcher) that a salesperson's value of outcomes that have happened in the past and his valence for the same set of outcomes which may happen in the future are very highly correlated. Finally, McClelland, et al., (1976) report that an individual's "need Achievement" orientation is learned by the onset of puberty and changes very little thereafter.

It is with the above evidence in mind that a test of the concurrent validity of the previously stated propositions was warranted. In short, the researcher feels justified in attempting to explain past salesperson performance by measuring the various psychological constructs relevant to the focal salesperson in the present time. In doing this, the researcher explicitly makes the assumption that the focal salesperson's "needs" and "valences" do not change appreciably throughout the time period that the salesperson has occupied his sales position.

One final note to make concerns the concurrent validation of Hypothesis Four, a hypothesis concerning an "expectancy" term. Though "expectancy" is a term concerning an individual's cognitive assessment of the probability that given events might take place in the future, the researcher felt that salespersons probably set personal sales production goals which are of equivalent difficulty, from year to year. Stemming from this assumed degree of invariance of the expectancy of personal goal fulfillment of a salesperson's personal sales goal from year to year is the notion that the expectancy of fulfillment of a salesperson's personal sales goal for the coming year will be roughly equal to the expectancy of fulfillment of a personal sales goal which the salesperson had at the beginning of the year for which sales production figures were gathered.

It is with the above notions in hand that concurrent validation of Hypothesis Four is being sought, a hypothesis which could normally be validated in a predictive sense.

3.4 Constructs to be Measured and Scales to be Used

Five sets of psychological constructs were measured within the context of this study. A description of these constructs will be given in the following pages. The characteristics of the scales used to measure the constructs, reported in prior published research, are given in the Appendix, page 122.

1. The valence, instrumentality and expectancy (VIE) constructs which are relevant to the formulation of a Vroomian motivational force score and which were used in this study are equivalent or identical to those constructs used in Oliver (1974), with one exception, which is noted below.
    a) Valence
    The "valence" score which is used represents the focal salesperson's affective valuation of what Vroom (1964) calls "second level outcomes". "Second level outcomes" are the outcomes which stem from the salesperson's performance on the job. ("Performance on the job" is what Vroom calls a "first level outcome".) Examples of second level outcomes are "pay", "promotion" and "prestige". Table 5 gives a list of the outcomes which will be used and how they are scored. In Table 6, the format is given which allowed the respondent to choose the five most important job outcomes. The use made of this information is detailed in Chapter 3.
    b) Expectancy
    The "expectancy" construct which is used in this study differs from the "expectancy" construct which has been used in other studies of salesperson motivation employing variations of Vroom's model (Oliver, 1974). In this study, the "expectancy" term refers to the focal salesperson's perceived probability of achieving his (her) own personal sales goal, not the perceived probability of achieving his sales quota. There are several reasons behind for doing this.
    i) If the members of sales management of the companies to be used in this study characteristically set quotas which are relatively easy to achieve, then one may encounter a "restriction of range" problem. In this case, many, if not most, of the salespersons might assign an "expectancy" value very close (or equal) to 1.0. In this case, "expectancy" would need to be factored out as a basically non-useful variable.
    ii) Another reason why one should use "expectancy" as the perceived probability of achieving one's own personal sales goal rather than the perceived probability of fulfilling one's sales quota stems from the notion that "fulfilling quota" has implications for the salespersons which may not relate to the psychological motivational "structure"

of the salesperson. According to Darmon (1974), the salesperson compensation scheme and its accompanying quota system fulfill at least three different functions: remunerating efforts of the salesperson; motivating the salesperson to perform on the job; and channeling the efforts of the salesperson. Thus, when a salesperson assigns a value for "expectancy" relative to "making quota", the salesperson's motivational perceptions may be influenced or confounded by the channeling aspects of the quota system.

For example, Darmon (1974) describes the results of a natural experiment wherein the salesperson incentive and quota-setting systems of a company were changed so as to give the members of the salesforce a greater share of the sales that they generate. The presumption was that salespersons would be "income maximizers" and that each salesperson would work harder to sell more than before in order to increase his income by a more than proportional amount.

Such was not the case, however. While some salespersons, did, in fact, increase their efforts, others decreased their efforts on the job. It follows, then, that one may not rightfully make simplifying assumptions concerning the probable ways in which a salesperson will be motivated to perform on the job by a quota.

The upshot of this discussion is that the "expectancy" of a salesperson achieving his quota has motivational implications which are currently not understandable.

Such appears not to be the case, however, with the "expectancy" of achieving one's own personal goal. As was suggested in the first chapter of this proposal, the works of Atkinson (1958) make precise performance predictions as a function of (1) the difficulty of the task (where "difficulty" of the task is the probability of successful task accomplishment ("expectancy"), and (2) the focal person's "need Achievement" score.

One may ask why the Atkinson framework may not work when the "expectancy" term is applied to the probability of "achieving quota". The reasons are twofold:

First, the effects of the "channeling" aspects of a quota may confound the predictions which one would want to make about the "motivating" aspects of the quota. One would suspect that there would be far fewer "channeling" effects present when one assesses the motivating aspects of one's own "personal sales goal".

Secondly, Atkinson's theory is operant only when the events for which an "expectancy" assessment is being made are in what Lewin (1938) would call the salesperson's "phenomenological" field of view. Here, the phenomenological field of view is similar to the notion of the "evoked set" which is frequently used in consumer behavior research. If one is assessing the motivational force which results from an outstanding salesperson's perceptions of his probability of "achieving quota", this event may not even be in the "phenomenological" field of view of the salesperson. The event which "making quota" constitutes might be a trivial one in that its accomplishment would be a forgone conclusion and would thus provide no motivational impetus for the outstanding salesperson.

    iii) Finally, defining "expectancy" in relation to one's own personal goal allows the researcher the opportunity to compare the three main theories of motivation, as was suggested in the first chapter. Specifically, the researcher is afforded the chance to investigate whether or not the "challenge" of a job (as measured by "expectancy" in this study) has a motivating effect on the salesperson which is independent of the rewards stemming from job performance. If there is an independent effect—and all three theories posit specific and disparate effects—then the results of the study may shed light as to which one of the three theories applies in this circumstance.

        Appendix page 120 details the implementation of the "expectancy" construct in the questionnaire format. (Information concerning the "perceived probability of achieving quota" will also be gathered, as is indicated on appendix page 121. Comparative empirical tests concerning the performance-capabilities of each of these three constructs have been conducted to determine if the proposed definition of "expectancy"—vis à vis "personal sales goal"—was, in fact, superior in a predictive sense to "expectancy" defined relative to "sales quota".)

c) Instrumentality

    The "instrumentality" construct used in this study is precisely analogous to the "instrumentality" construct described and used in other empirical research concerning salesperson motivation and performance (Oliver, 1974; Churchill, Ford and Walker, 1976). The "instrumentality" construct is defined as a conditional probability variable. Two applications of "instrumentality" are to be implemented: one use refers to the salesperson's perceived conditional relationship between achieving sales quota and receiving job outcomes (rewards). The other involves the relationship between the attainment of the salesperson's "personal sales goal" and the reception of job outcomes. The formal definition of "instrumentality" is as follows: "instrumentality" is defined as the probability perceived by the salesperson that attaining sales quota (personal sales goal) will lead to the reception of job outcomes (rewards).

For each of the 17 outcomes listed in Table 5, there are two instrumentality figures given. For a given outcome, Table 7 relates the salesperson's perceived probability that attaining his sales quota will allow him to receive that job outcome. Correspondingly, the figure in Table 8 relates the salesperson's perceived probability that his attaining his personal sales goal will lead to his receiving the outcome in question.

2. Job scope variables.

   The "job scope" variables to be used in this study were nearly identical to the ones originally developed and reported by Hackman and Oldham (1975). The only changes which are made are ones which result from adapting the items so that they are pertinent to sales activities rather than management activities. Table 9 details the structuring of the questions which probe the "job scope" issues.

3. The MNQ "need Achievement" variable which is used in this study will be one of the two n Ach scales used. This variable is given in Table 10.

4. An additional scale for "need Achievement".

   Due to the central position that "need Achievement" plays in this study, and in light of the fact that the scale for "n Ach" that Steers and Braunstein (1976) designed has only 5 items, it is felt that having a "back-up" scale for "n Ach" would help to provide increased reliability for the results. A good candidate for this scale can be found in Jackson's Personality Research Form (Jackson, 1967). This inventory has been used widely in the literature in the past (Steers and Braunstein, 1976) and has been proven to contain a very valid and reliable scale for measuring "need Achievement". Table 11 gives the items which constitute this scale.

5. Task-goal attributes.

   The Task-Goal Attribute Questionnaire (TGAQ) developed by Steers (1976) was used in determining whether or not the variables which are operant in a Management by Objectives program are associated with good performance on the job. In addition, tests were conducted to determine if a "need Achievement"-moderated relationship existed between these variables and the performance variables. Chapter 4 details the results of these analyses. Table 12 indicates the nature of this scale as it was implemented for these analyses.

6. Biographical information.

   The biographical information to be gathered is outlined in Table 13.

7. Performance data.

   Salesperson performance measurements constitute a major topic and are the subject of the next section.

3.5 The Performance Measures

The nature of the salesperson performance measure deserves special consideration, for several reasons. These are as follows:

1. Until very recently, there has been no research method discussed in the literature which can be used to adjust or covary out the biasing effects of variables such as "salesperson territory potential" and "salesperson territory geographical dispersion" on the sales performance of a salesperson (Ryans and Weinberg, 1978).
2. There is no universally accepted univariate measure of sales performance (Behrman and Perreault, 1978).

In addressing the need alluded to in 1. above, Ryans and Weinberg (1978) offer a procedure which allows the researcher to adjust for the biasing effects of the following variables, which differ from one salesperson to the next.

1. The "span of control" of the district manager overseeing the focal salesperson.
2. The sales potential of the focal salesperson's territory.
3. The geographic dispersion of the focal salesperson's territory.
4. The experience of the focal salesperson in his present position.

Given directly below are summary descriptions of the reasons how these variables may introduce bias into the measurement of the job performance of a salesperson. Following this is a description of the procedure which Ryans and Weinberg suggest to statistically remove the bias introduced by these four variables.

3.5.1 *Span of Control of the District Manager*

The greater the span of control of the district manager, the greater the number of salespersons whom the district manager must oversee and the lesser is the time which the district manager can devote to each salesperson for management purposes. Ryans and Weinberg (1978) present evidence making this point. Latham and Yukl (1975) also present a similar reasoning, indicating that "close supervision" (presumably stemming from a smaller "span of control") will increase employee performance.

3.5.2 *Sales Territory Potential*

It is relatively easy to see the reasoning behind the notion that the greater the sales territory potential, the greater the sales which will be forthcoming from a given sales effort (ceteris paribus).

Lucas, Weinberg and Clowes (1975), Cravens, Woodruff and Stamper (1972) and Bagozzi (1976) provide ample evidence to this effect.

3.5.3 Sales Territory Dispersion

One might imagine that the larger the territory a salesperson covers, the greater the non-productive "travel time" that the salesperson must engage in, and the less the productive "calling time" will be available to the salesperson. Lucas, Weinberg and Clowes (1975) and Ryans and Weinberg (1978) give empirical evidence which suggests that "sales territory dispersion" is negatively associated with "sales".

3.5.4 Salesperson Experience

Also intuitively compelling is the notion that a salesperson's experience is a factor which has an independent positive effect on the salesperson's sales record. Cravens and Woodruff (1973) and Beswick and Cravens (1977) empirically verify this positive relationship.

Table 4 contains the operational definitions of the above four variables. The procedure by which information on these variables was used to remove bias is described below.

The procedure for determining the biasing effects of the previously mentioned four variables on a salesperson's job performance involves several steps (Ryans and Weinberg, 1978). These steps are given below. Symbolically, one has

estimated sales for salesperson "i" =
alpha(est) × exp((S"i") × (E"i") × (P"i") × (D"i")),

where S"i", E"i", P"i" and D"i" are the focal salesperson's "score" on the "span", "experience", "potential" and "dispersion" variables, respectively.

This estimate represents the average sales figure which one would expect to be generated when an individual registers the scores on the four variables S, E, P and D which are of the magnitude S"i", E"i", P"i", and D"i". The figure thus derived will constitute the measure of the salesperson's performance with the biasing effects of span, experience, sales potential and geographic dispersion removed.

Please note, however, that this estimate is a function only of the scores S"i", E"i", P"i" and D"i" of salesperson "i". In order to use this estimate in conjunction with the information to be gathered on the previously described psychological constructs, the following procedure is recommended: Define an adjusted sales figure as

Sales(adjusted) for salesperson "i" = Sales(actual) "i" + Residual "i"

where,

> Sales(actual) "i" = actual sales registered by the focal salesperson "i" and,
>
> Residual "i" = the residual figure which results from regressing "sales" on "span", "experience", "potential" and "dispersion".

This adjusted sales figure is positive when the salesperson is performing better than the company's average salesperson operating at his (the focal salesperson's) specific levels of span of control, territory sales potential, dispersion and salesperson experience. Conversely, a negative score indicates that the salesperson's selling activity is below the company average, given his specific score on these variables.

As a check on the estimation procedure above, the sales supervisor was asked to give a subjective performance evaluation of the focal salesperson, taking into account such issues as the salesperson's age, experience with the company and territory potential. This second measure of a salesperson's performance, then, is a subjective evaluation on the part of the district manager with respect to the focal salesperson's overall performance, with the issues above being held constant.

A third measure—a salesperson's performance vs. quota—also provides a validity check on the first measure of a salesperson's performance given.

A fourth performance measure—"sales" only—will be given for two reasons:

1. The results generated in this study can be compared with the results of other empirical studies of salesperson motivation and performance; and

2. The covariates to be used in the first measure of a salesperson's performance may, for unforseeable reasons idiosyncratic to this study, prove not to be of use.

Given below is a summary of the four univariate performance measures. Taken as a unit, they will constitute the multivariate measure of salesperson performance in this study.

1. "Adjusted sales" of the focal salesperson, with the biasing effects of territory sales potential, et al., statistically removed—an objective measure.

2. "Sales" of the focal salesperson relative to quota—an objective measure.
3. "Sales"—an objective measure.
4. Overall performance of the focal salesperson in comparison with the other salespersons in his district, measured by the district manager—a subjective measure.

3.6 Data Analysis

This section deals with the specific statistical methodologies which will be used to analyze the data to be gathered from salespersons concerning the constructs described in the previous sections of this chapter. The analyses will broadly concern the concurrent validity of Hypotheses 1-4, ones which were described in previous sections of this chapter.

Hypothesis One: A two-part hypothesis.

1. The salesperson's valence for achieving his sales quota, defined as,

    Valence for achieving quota $= \sum_{i=1}^{r} I"i" \times V"i"$,

    is positively related with the salesperson's performance.
    $V"i"$ = the salesperson's valence for outcome "i" (Table 5), and $I"i"$ = the salesperson's perceived instrumentality that achieving his sales quota will have for receiving outcome "i" (Table 7 and Table 8).

2. The salesperson's valence for achieving his personal sales goal, defined as:

    Valence for attaining one's personal sales goal $= \sum_{i=1}^{r} I"j" \times V"j"$

    is positively related with the salesperson's performance, where $V"j"$ and $I"j"$ are the instrumentality and valence perceptions relative to the salesperson achieving his personal sales goal (see Table 8).

The general form of the two parts of Hypothesis One is one which is roughly equivalent to Galbraith and Cumming's (1967). The hypothesis given above differs from that posited by Galbraith and Cummings theory in that "performance" is explicitly defined as:

1. Achieving one's sales quota (in Hypothesis One-part one); and

2. Achieving one's own personal sales goal (in Hypothesis One-part two).

No such explicit definition of "performance" is made in Galbraith and Cummings (1967).

The correlational procedure being proposed here is somewhat different than the one employed by Galbraith and Cummings. Each of the four univariate measures will be singly regressed against the "valence for achieving quota" and "valence for achieving one's own personal sales goal" variables, where each of the latter two variables generates a single aggregated figure. In Galbraith and Cummings, a single performance measure is regressed against seven (Instrumentality × Valence) combinations in a disaggregated fashion.

The above distinction of aggregation vs. disaggregation brings up another point. In this study, not all of the 17 outcomes presented to each salesperson (given in Table 5) enter into the calculation of the "valence for achieving quota/goal" scores for the individual salesperson observation. Having each salesperson choose a subset of the outcomes which are listed in Table 6 as the set of outcomes having the most influence on the performance of the focal salesperson on the job will enable the researcher to choose the "salient set" of job outcomes for the focal salesperson. Using this subset of job outcomes for making aggregated calculations of "valence" (for making "quota" or "personal goal", for instance) is a procedure which several authors (Bem, 1970; Fishbein, 1967; Hansen, 1969; and Rosenberg, 1956) indicate improves the predictive capability of linear compensatory models. The presumption is that the number of outcomes which are motivationally "salient" to the focal salesperson is small. Hansen (1969) and others suggest three to five job outcomes as constituting an optimal number of outcomes to enter into the calculations.

The correlational procedure, then, is conducted as each of the five univariate performance scores, alluded to previously, are regressed against each of the "valence for achieving quota" and "valence for achieving one's personal goal" scores. Hypothesis One would be at least partially confirmed if a significant Pearson product/moment correlation were to be found between either aggregated "valence" score and any of the four performance scores.

3.7 Methodological Advances for Testing Hypothesis One

In this proposal, the researcher is proposing the implementation of a methodological advance which appears to offer promise for increasing the precision with which one can test the two parts of Hypothesis One. This advance is given below.

> Divide each "outcome" and each "instrumentality" response of each salesperson by the standard deviation of the responses exhibited by the salesperson in responding to all of the items in the "outcome" and "instrumentality" sets, respectively.

Elaborations on the above methodological improvement are given below.

In Oliver's study, which represented the initial application of a Vroomian model for predicting job performance in a salesforce context (Oliver, 1974), note was made of the fact that none of the Pearson product/moment correlations between either of his two performance variables and any of the motivational "force" scores exceeded .5. That is, the maximum coefficient of determination ("R squared") generated in Oliver's study was approximately .25. Oliver attributed the low correlations achieved to what he called the "heterogeneity of respondents" used in the study. Though Oliver did not in any direct way specify a definition of this term, this researcher has deduced from readings in the literature concerning the application of linear compensatory models in consumer attitudinal research that there is at least one possible source of "heterogeneity of respondents":

> The notion that individuals exhibit differing dispersions (standard deviations) of responses in assigning their own scores on the "valence" for outcomes and "instrumentality" measures.

The source of "heterogeneity of respondents" given above is the target of the methodological refinement alluded to in this section. Restated below is the procedure which addresses the source of "heterogeneity of respondents".

> Divide each salesperson's "valence" for job outcome and "instrumentality" responses by the standard deviations exhibited by the responses in the entire "valence" for job outcome and "instrumentality" sets, respectively.

Bass and Wilkie (1973) state very succinctly the problem which occurs when individuals exhibit differing response "dispersions" in assigning scores to constructs used in linear attitude models:

> "Unweighted variables summed into a composite weight themselves in proportion to their standard deviations."

In this situation, the statement implies that if an individual's responses on the "valence" for job outcomes questions exhibit a higher standard deviation than the dispersion which he exhibits in responding to "instrumentality" items, then the "valence" component of the expression,

$$\sum_{i=1}^{r} Ii\ Vi$$

will receive a greater weight than will the "instrumentality" component.

One might rightfully conjecture at this point as to what the manifestations of this imbalance in weighting between the two constructs are. Sheth and Talarzyk (1972) and Churchill (1972) reported results of studies which would indicate that the raw scores on the "valence" construct would act as "suppressors" on the predictive capabilities of the "instrumentality" constructs.

Bass and Wilkie (1973) demonstrate that the "suppressor" effect disappears if one standardizes the valence and instrumentality variables prior to summing the products into a composite. Symbolically, one would have:

Valence for Attaining Personal Goal/Quota
$$= \Sigma \, I(\text{Normalized}) \times V(\text{Normalized})$$
$$= \Sigma \, I(\text{normalized}) \times V(\text{normalized}) \text{ quota}$$

When Bass and Wilkie used this normalizing procedure on the data used in Sheth and Talarzyk (1973), they show that the use of this procedure more than doubles the coefficient of determination which Sheth and Talarzyk had previously reported.

Mitchell (1974), however, reports that the use of a pure standardization procedure in motivational research using some variation of Vroom's model is not justified. He asserts that when one standardizes the variables, then real differences in mean scores on the "valence" and "instrumentality" variables are lost (since standardization would entail having the mean "instrumentality" and "valence" scores set to 0).

It appears, however, that if one divides each individual's "valence" for outcomes and "instrumentality" scores by the standard deviation of the "valence" for outcomes and "instrumentality" sets of items, respectively, and does not adjust the means for each of these sets to 0, then one can achieve "homogeneity of respondents" with respect to response deviations (dispersions) without losing mean differences in these variables. (In a personal conversation with this researcher, Gilbert Churchill, Jr., said that the procedure advocated in this section should help to bring about the desired results.)

3.8 Test of the Importance of Job Scope Issues

The next hypothesis tested (Hypothesis Two) concerns the notion of whether or not knowledge of a salesperson's perceptions of job scope issues, in addition to knowledge of the valence and instrumentality issues, is of assistance to the researcher in predicting the job performance of the focal salesperson. The statistical techniques used in making this test are the univariate and multivariate analysis of covariance techniques (Winer, 1971). Appendix page 121 gives the specific set of linear models to be employed in determining whether or not the "job scope" variables are significant predictors of job performance, with the "valence for attaining sales quota" and "valence for attaining one's own personal sales goal" to be used as covariates.

3.8.1 Procedure for the Analysis

In the analysis, the two steps given below are followed for each of the dependent (performance) variables, designated Y"i" (i = 1 to 5):

STEP ONE: Test of the usefulness of the variables, (a) "valence for attaining sales quota" and (b) "valence for attaining one's own personal sales goal" as covariates for the job performance/job scope relationship. The test of the significance of the difference in the regression sums of squares between Model I "i" and Model II "i" is the test of whether or not the variable X(2) qualifies as a covariate. Correspondingly, the test of the significance of the difference in the regression sums of squares between Model I "i" and Model III "i" tests whether or not X(1) qualifies as a covariate. If either variable (or both variables) qualifies (qualify) as a covariate, then the qualifying variable(s) will be retained for further linear model testing.

STEP TWO: Test the usefulness of the "job scope" variables as predictors of criterion (performance) variable Y "i". The test of significance of the regression sums of squares of the difference between Model IV "i" and Model I "i" (if both covariates qualify) is the test of the usefulness of the "job scope" variables as predictors of criterion (performance) variable Y "i".

One may determine whether or not a significant relationship exists (moderated or otherwise) between the job scope variables (represented by the Motivational Potential Score) and the job performance variables by including both the MPS variable and the MPSX "need Achievement" interaction in the same regression equation, regressing each sales performance variable on these two variables. If each variable is significant eliminating the other variable, then the relationship is both significant and moderated.

The methodological approach used in testing Hypothesis Three is very similar to the methodology employed to test Hypothesis Two, and is given in the next section.

3.9 "Participation" as a Predictor of Sales Performance

As Steers (1976) indicates, the relationship between "participation in goal-setting" and "job performance" appears to be moderated by "need Achievement". Persons low in "n Ach" are presumably positively motivated to perform on the job by this type of participation, and high "n Ach" persons will presumably experience no change in motivation on the job by "participation in goal-setting".

The methodology to be used to test Hypothesis Three is the same as the methodology to be used to test Hypothesis Two. The only difference is that the "job scope" variables $X(k)$ ($k = 3$ to 8) are replaced by the "participation" variable $X(3)$.

The test of significance of "participation in goal-setting" involves first dividing the sample into persons high in "need Achievement" and persons low in "n Ach" and then seeing if the regression slope for the job performance/participation relationship is the same for high "n Ach" salespeople as for their low "n Ach" counterparts. If the slopes are the same, then there is no moderator effect. That is, if there is a significant participation X "n Ach" interaction, then there is a significant moderator effect. Also, the coefficient of the "participation" variable alone needs to be assessed for significance.

This completes the discussion concerning how one may test for the existence of a moderator effect for the "n Ach" variable with respect to the job performance-job scope and job performance-participation relationships.

3.10 Test of Hypothesis Four

The final hypothesis to be tested is an hypothesis which focuses upon the role which the "expectancy" variable plays in cognitive theories of motivation. This hypothesis is given below:

> HYPOTHESIS FOUR: When "expectancy" is defined as the "perceived probability of achieving one's own personal production goal", and when the "valence for attaining one's own personal sales goal" is used as a covariate, "need Achievement" moderates the relationship between "expectancy" and "sales performance".

The approach used to test Hypothesis Four is a two-step procedure:

> STEP ONE: Determine whether or not a significant relationship exists between "expectancy" and "sales performance" with "valence for attaining one's own personal sales goal" to be used as a covariate and with moderators present in the analysis.
> If a positive relationship exists then the empirical evidence will favor the theory of Vroom (1964), and Hypothesis Four will be rejected. If a negative relationship exists between "expectancy" and "sales performance", then the theory of Locke (1978) will gain confirmation, and Hypothesis Four will be rejected. If significant relationship exists, then one may proceed to step two of the process of testing Hypothesis Four.
>
> STEP TWO: Given that there is no significant unmoderated relationship between "expectancy" and "sales performance", test whether or not a "need Achievement"-moderated relationship exists between "expectancy" and "sales performance".

Test the equivalence of the regression slopes between the expectancy of achieving one's own personal sales goal and job performance for persons who are high in "n Ach" and persons who are low in "n Ach". If there is no moderator effect, then no motivational theory concerning "expectancy" will receive confirmation. If there is a moderator effect, then a test is made to ensure that the direction of the slopes is in line with the implications of the theory of "need Achievement" of Atkinson.

Table 4. Operational Definitions

VARIABLE	OPERATIONAL DEFINITION
Span of Control	Number of salespersons reporting to the first level sales manager responsible for the sales territory
Salesperson Experience	Number of months with the company in the present territory
Territory Potential	Estimate in the denominations of of product sold
Territory dispersion	Area in square miles

Table 5. Section Probing Job Outcomes

INSTRUCTIONS

The rewards, or, more generally speaking, the "outcomes" which salesperson receives from functioning in his or her job are many and varied in nature. "Pay" and "promotion" are two "outcomes" which come from doing one's job well. "Feeling more secure on the job" is another "outcome" which may stem from the successful accomplishment of one's sales objectives.

Given on the next page are 17 job "outcomes" which a salesperson may receive or experience as a result of performing on the job. Though most of these "outcomes" are desirable in nature, several may be classified aas undesirable. Please place a check mark on the line under that word or phrase which best describes your feelings about receiving or experiencing that outcome.

For example,

Suppose that doing well in sales in your company will enable you to receive a free "country club" membership. Assume that you feel basically indifferent toward receiving this outcome. Then you would mark your answer as follows:

Very Undesirable	Somewhat Undesirable	Indifferent	Somewhat Desirable	Very Desirable
-----	-----	__X__	-----	-----

Please go on to the next page and complete this section.

Very Undesirable	Somewhat Undesirable	Indifferent	Somewhat Desirable	Very Desirable

___1. Receiving more responsibility in my position

----- ----- ----- ----- -----

___2. Getting improvements in home office practices and procedures

_____   _____   _____   _____   _____

___3. Having better working relations with my supervisor

_____   _____   _____   _____   _____

___4. Furthering my professional growth and development

_____   _____   _____   _____   _____

___5. Receiving more recognition and appreciation for my production efforts

_____   _____   _____   _____   _____

___6. Getting better office facilities

_____   _____   _____   _____   _____

___7. Feeling more secure in my job

_____   _____   _____   _____   _____

___8. Feeling more secure in my job

_____   _____   _____   _____   _____

___9. Advancing within the company to a higher field management position

_____   _____   _____   _____   _____

___10. Receiving more income from my job

_____   _____   _____   _____   _____

Very Undesirable	Somewhat Undesirable	Indifferent	Somewhat Desirable	Very Desirable

___11. Making greater use of my skills and abilities on my job

___ ___ ___ ___ ___

___12. Having my family and friends view my job as having greater prestiege

___ ___ ___ ___ ___

___13. Getting better supervision

___ ___ ___ ___ ___

___14. Feeling greater self-esteem from my job

___ ___ ___ ___ ___

___15. Going to sales conventions and meetings

___ ___ ___ ___ ___

___16. Having better working relations with the other salespeople in my company

___ ___ ___ ___ ___

___17. Being away from my family for extended periods of time

___ ___ ___ ___ ___

___ 18. Feeling a greater sense of self-fulfillment from
        my job

    _____   _____   _____   _____   _____

        WHEN YOU HAVE FINISHED MARKING ALL OF THE ITEMS ABOVE,
        PLEASE GO ON TO THE NEXT PAGE.

Table 6. Choice of Important Job Outcomes

Now that you have finished marking how you feel about
various job outcomes (given on the previous two pages)
please go BACK to these items and choose the 5 items
which have the GREATEST IMPACT on your job
performance (whether favorably or unfavorably).
For each of these five most influential items,
place a check mark on the line just to the left of
the item number.

As an example, suppose that "making more friends" was
an outcome listed in the items on the previous two
pages, and that this was the 25th item listed (even
though, in reality, there are only 17 items listed).
If this were one of your five MOST INFLUENTIAL OUTCOMES,
then you would place a check mark as follows.

_x_25.   Making more friends

WHEN YOU HAVE FINISHED MARKING YOUR FIVE MOST INFLUENTIAL
CHOICES, PLEASE GO ON TO THE NEXT SECTION.

Table 7. Instrumentalities of Attaining the Sales Quota

In this section, you will be asked to describe your
perceptions of the extent to which your achieving
your SALES QUOTA will
enable you to receive each of the job outcomes
which were previously assessed.

In this section, you will NOT be asked to again rate
the desirability of the outcomes. Rather, please
give your best estimate, using the "chances out of 100"
notation, that your ACHIEVING YOUR SALES QUOTA will
lead to your receiving EACH of the 17 outcomes,
previously listed.

For example, suppose that ACHIEVING YOUR SALES QUOTA
would PROBABLY enable you to receive a free trip
to the Bahamas. Then your best estimate of your
"chances out of 100" of your achieving sales quota
LEADING TO "receiving a trip to the Bahamas" might
be 70 out of 100, or ".7", in short.

Your answer would appear as follows:

.1   .2   .3   .4   .5   .6   .7   .8   .9   1.0

Receiving a
free trip to
the B'hmas   ___ ___ ___ ___ ___ ___ _X_ ___ ___ ___

Please complete this section when you understand the instructions.

.1   .2   .3   .4   .5   .6   .7   .8   .9   1.0

Receiving more responsibility in my position

___ ___ ___ ___ ___ ___ ___ ___ ___ ___

Getting improvements in home office practices and procedures

--- --- --- --- --- --- --- --- --- ---

Having better working relations with my supervisor

--- --- --- --- --- --- --- --- --- ---

.1 .2 .3 .4 .5 .6 .7 .8 .9 1.0

Furthering my professional growth and development

--- --- --- --- --- --- --- --- --- ---

Receiving more recognition and appreciation for my efforts

--- --- --- --- --- --- --- --- --- ---

Getting better office facilities

--- --- --- --- --- --- --- --- --- ---

.1 .2 .3 .4 .5 .6 .7 .8 .9 1.0

Feeling more secure in my job

--- --- --- --- --- --- --- --- --- ---

Feeling a greater sense of accomplishment from the work that I am doing

--- --- --- --- --- --- --- --- --- ---

Advancing within the company to a (higher) field
management position

___ ___ ___ ___ ___ ___ ___ ___ ___ ___
.1 .2 .3 .4 .5 .6 .7 .8 .9 1.0

Receiving more income from my job

___ ___ ___ ___ ___ ___ ___ ___ ___ ___

Making greater use of my skills and abilities on my
job
sk 2 a

___ ___ ___ ___ ___ ___ ___ ___ ___ ___

Having my family and friends view my job as having
reater prestiege

___ ___ ___ ___ ___ ___ ___ ___ ___ ___
.1 .2 .3 .4 .5 .6 .7 .8 .9 1.0

Getting better supervision

___ ___ ___ ___ ___ ___ ___ ___ ___ ___

Feeling greater self-esteem from my job

___ ___ ___ ___ ___ ___ ___ ___ ___ ___

Going to sales conventions and meetings

___ ___ ___ ___ ___ ___ ___ ___ ___ ___

Having better working relations with the other salespeople
in my company

___ ___ ___ ___ ___ ___ ___ ___ ___ ___

Being away from my family for extended periods of time

　　　　　　.1　.2　.3　.4　.5　.6　.7　.8　.9　1.0

Feeling a greater sense of fulfillment from my job

Table 8.　Instrumentalities of the Personal Goal

In this section, you will be asked to describe your perceptions of the extent to which your achieving your OWN PERSONAL SALES GOAL (referred to in section H) will enable you to RECEIVE each of the job outcomes which were previously assessed for the desirability in a previous section.

In this section, you will NOT be asked to again rate the desirability of the outcomes. Rather, please give your best estimate, using the "chances out of 100" notation, that your achieving your PERSONAL SALES GOAL (NOT quota) will lead to your receiving EACH of the 17 outcomes, previously listed in Section C and listed again below.

For example, suppose that achieving your PERSONAL SALES GOAL would ALMOST CERTAINLY enable you to receive the free trip to the Bahamas mentioned in the previous section. Then your best estimate of your "chances out of 100" of your achieving your personal sales goal LEADING TO "receiving a free trip to the Bahamas" would probably be in the neighborhood of 90 out of 100, or ".9", in short.

Your answer would appear as follows:

　　　　　　　　.1　.2　.3　.4　.5　.6　.7　.8　.9　1.0

Receiving a
free trip to
the B'hmas　　　___ ___ ___ ___ ___ ___ ___ ___ _X_ ___

Please complete the balance of this section.

Having better working relations with my supervisor

--- --- --- --- --- --- --- --- --- ---

Furthering my professional growth and development

--- --- --- --- --- --- --- --- --- ---

Getting improvements in home office practices and procedures

--- --- --- --- --- --- --- --- --- ---

.1 .2 .3 .4 .5 .6 .7 .8 .9 1.0

Receiving more recognition and appreciation for my efforts

--- --- --- --- --- --- --- --- --- ---

Receiving more responsibility in my postition

--- --- --- --- --- --- --- --- --- ---

Getting better office facilities

--- --- --- --- --- --- --- --- --- ---

.1 .2 .3 .4 .5 .6 .7 .8 .9 1.0

Receiving more income from my job

--- --- --- --- --- --- --- --- --- ---

Having my family and friends view my job as having
greater prestiege

--- --- --- --- --- --- --- --- --- ---

Feeling a greater sense of accomplishment from the work
that I am doing

--- --- --- --- --- --- --- --- --- ---

.1 .2 .3 .4 .5 .6 .7 .8 .9 1.0

Feeling more secure in my job

--- --- --- --- --- --- --- --- --- ---

Making greater use of my skills and abilities on my job

--- --- --- --- --- --- --- --- --- ---

Advancing within the company to a (higher) field
management position

--- --- --- --- --- --- --- --- --- ---

.1 .2 .3 .4 .5 .6 .7 .8 .9 1.0

Being away from my family for long periods of time

--- --- --- --- --- --- --- --- --- ---

Getting better supervision

--- --- --- --- --- --- --- --- --- ---

Feeling a greater sense of fulfillment from my job

--- --- --- --- --- --- --- --- --- ---

.1 .2 .3 .4 .5 .6 .7 .8 .9 1.0

Going to sales conventions and meetings

___ ___ ___ ___ ___ ___ ___ ___ ___ ___

Having better working relations with the other salespeople
in my company

___ ___ ___ ___ ___ ___ ___ ___ ___ ___

Feeling greater self-esteem from my job

___ ___ ___ ___ ___ ___ ___ ___ ___ ___

YOU HAVE FINISHED THIS SECTION. PLEASE GO ON TO THE NEXT SECTION.

Table 9. Scale for Job Scope Variables

DIRECTIONS: In this part of the questionnaire you are asked to describe as OBJECTIVELY as you can various aspects of your job. Please do NOT use this part of the questionnaire to show how much you like or dislike your job. Instead, try to make your descriptions as accurate and as objective as is possible.

A sample question is given below.

A. To what extent does your job require you to work with mechanical equipment?

1-------2-------3-------4-------5-------6-------7

| Very little; the job requires almost no contact with mechanical equip. | Moderately | Very much; the job requires almost constant work with mechanical equipment |

description of your job.

If, for example, your job requires you to work with mechanical equipment a good deal of the time--but also requires some paperwork--you might circle the number six (6), as was done in the example above.

WHEN YOU UNDERSTAND THE ABOVE INSTRUCTIONS, PLEASE COMPLETE THE ITEMS GIVEN IN THE SECTION BELOW.

1. How much AUTONOMY is there in your job? That is, to what extent does your job permit you to decide ON YOUR OWN how to go about doing the work?

1-------2-------3-------4-------5-------6-------7

| Very little; the job gives me almost no personal "say" about how and when the work is done. | Moderate Autonomy many things are standardized and not under my control, but I can make some decisions about the work. | Very little; the job gives me almost complete responsibility for deciding how and when the work is done |

Research Methods   67

2. To what extent does your job involve doing a "WHOLE" and identifiable sales job? That is, is the job a complete piece of work that has an obvious beginning and end? Or is it only a small part of the overall selling job, which is finished by other people who are part of a "sales team"?

1--------2--------3--------4---------5--------6---------7

| My job is only a tiny part of the overall selling activities cannot be seen from the final sale. | My job is a moderate-sized chunk of the overall selling activities. My own contribution can be seen in the final outcome of the sales effort. | My job involves doing the whole selling activity, from start to finish; the results of my activities are easily seen in the final outcome of the sales effort. |

3. How much VARIETY is there in your job? That is, to what extent does the job require you to do many different things at work, using a variety of your skills and talents?

1--------2--------3---------4---------5---------6---------7

| Very little; the job requires me to do the same routine things over and over again. | Moderate variety | Very Much; the job requires me to do many different things, using a number of different skills and talents. |

4. In general, how SIGNIFICANT OR IMPORTANT is your job? That is, are the results of your work likely to significantly affect the lives or well-being of other people?

1---------2----------3----------4----------5----------6---------7

| Not very significant; the outcomes of my work are NOT likely to have important effects on other people. | Moderately Significant | Highly significant the outcomes of my work can affect other people in very important way |

5. To what extent does DOING THE JOB ITSELF provide you with information about your work performance? That is, does the

actual WORK ITSELF provide clues about how well you are doing--aside from any feedback which co-workers or supervisors may provide?

1---------2---------3---------4---------5---------6--------7

Very little; the job itself is set up so that I could work forever without finding out how well I am doing.

Moderately ; sometimes doing the job provides "feedback" to me; sometimes it does not

Very much; the job is set up so that I get almost const "feedback" as I wo about how well I a doing.

WHEN YOU HAVE FINISHED ANSWERING ALL OF THE ITEMS IN THIS SECTION, PLEASE GO ON TO THE NEXT SECTION.

DIRECTIONS: Listed below are a number of statements which coul be used to describe a job. You are to indicate whether each statement is an ACCURATE or an INACCURATE description of YOUR job. Once again, please try to be as objective as you can in deciding how accurately each statement describes your job--

PLEASE GO ON TO THE NEXT SECTION WHEN YOU UNDERSTAND THE ABOVE INSTRUCTIONS.

Write a number in the blank beside each statement, based on the following scale:

HOW ACCURATE IS THE STATEMENT IN DESCRIBING YOUR JOB ?

1	2	3	4	5	6	
Very Inaccurate	Mostly Inaccur.	Slightly Inaccur.	Uncertain	Slightly Accurate	Mostly Accur.	Ver Accu

_____1. The job requires me to use a number of complex or high-level skills.

_____2. The job is arranged so that I do NOT have the chance to do an entire selling job from beginning to end.

_____3. Just doing the work required by the job provides many chances for me to figure out how well I am doing.

_____4. The job is simple and repetitive.

_____5. The job is one where a lot of people can be affected by how well the job gets done.

_____6. The job denies me any chance to use my personal initiative or judgment in carrying out the work.

_____7. The job provides me the chance to completely finish the pieces of work that I begin.

_____8. The job itself provides very few clues about whether or not I am performing the job well.

_____9. The job gives me considerable opportunity for independence and freedom in how I do the work.

____10. The job itself is NOT very significant or important in the broader scheme of things.

WHEN YOU HAVE FINISHED ANSWERING ALL OF THE ITEMS IN THIS SECTION, PLEASE GO ON THE NEXT SECTION.

Table 10. Manifest Needs Questionnaire

INSTRUCTIONS

In this section are listed 20 statements that describe various things that salespeople do at work. Please place a check mark on the line under that word or phrase which best describes your own actions on the job.

Some of the items in the inventory may appear to be similar to you. Again, do not try to remember how you checked similar items in this section. Make each item a separate and independent judgment, and work as quickly and as carefully as is possible.

As an example:

Suppose that you feel that the sales territories which you have had in the past have ALWAYS been too small; you would place a check mark (or cross mark) as follows:

Strongly Agree	Agree	Neither Agree nor Disagree	Disagree	Strongly Disagree

My sales territories have been too small.

__x__	_____	_____	_____	_____

Now, proceed to the next page and answer all of the items in this section. Remember, it is your "first impressions" that we want.

Strongly Agree	Agree	Neither Agree nor Disagree	Disagree	Strongly Disagree

1. I do my best work when my sales assignments are fairly difficult.

_____	_____	_____	_____	_____

2. When I have a choice, I try too work in a group instead of by myself.

   _____   _____   _____   _____   _____

3. In my sales assignments, I try to be my own boss.

   _____   _____   _____   _____   _____

4. I seek an active role in the leadership of a group.

   _____   _____   _____   _____   _____

5. I try very hard to improve on my past sales performance.

   _____   _____   _____   _____   _____

6. I pay a good deal of attention to the feelings of others in my work.

   _____   _____   _____   _____   _____

7. I go my own way at work, regardless of the opinions of others.

   _____   _____   _____   _____   _____

8. I avoid trying to influence those around me to see things my way.

   _____   _____   _____   _____   _____

9. I take moderate risks and stick my neck out to get ahead at work.

   _____   _____   _____   _____   _____

10. I prefer to do my own work and let others do theirs.

    _____   _____   _____   _____   _____

Strongly Agree	Agree	Neither Agree nor Disagree	Disagree	Strongly Disagree

11. I disregard rules and regulations which hamper my personal freedom.

_____   _____   _____   _____   _____

12. I find myself organizing and directing the activities of others.

_____   _____   _____   _____   _____

13. I try to avoid any added responsibilities on the job.

_____   _____   _____   _____   _____

14. I express my disagreements with others openly.

_____   _____   _____   _____   _____

15. I consider myself a "team player" at work.

_____   _____   _____   _____   _____

16. I strive to gain more control over the events around me at work.

_____   _____   _____   _____   _____

17. I try to perform better than my fellow salespersons.

_____   _____   _____   _____   _____

18. I find myself talking to those around me about non-business related matters.

_____   _____   _____   _____   _____

Strongly Agree	Agree	Neither Agree nor Disagree	Disagree	Strongly Disagree

19. I try my best to work alone on a job.

_____   _____   _____   _____   _____

20. I strive to be "in command" when I am working in a group.

_____   _____   _____   _____   _____

YOU HAVE FINISHED THIS SECTION. PLEASE GO ON TO THE NEXT SECTION.

Table 11. The Jackson Preference Scale for "Need Achievement"

		Strongly		Neither Agree nor		Strongly
1.	I know exactly what I want out of life	-------	-----	---------	---------	--------
2.	In general I try to make every minute count	-------	-----	---------	---------	--------
3.	I often find myself doing or saying something for the pleasure of it, rather than because it serves a purpose	------	-----	---------	---------	--------
4.	I almost always feel that I must do the best at what I am doing	------	-----	---------	---------	--------
5.	I try harder to be content with myself than to be successful	-----	-----	--------	--------	---------
6.	Every day I try to accomplish something worthwhile	-----	----	--------	--------	---------
7.	I always try to do my best, whether I am alone or with someone.	-----	-----	---------	--------	---------

Table 12. Task-Goal Attribute Questionnaire

INSTRUCTIONS

Listed below is a set of statements which may or may
not describe your own job objectives toward which
you are presently working. Please reaad each
statement carefully and then place a check mark
on the line above one of the five alternatives which
best describes your degree of agreement or
disagreement with the statement. PLEASE ANSWER ALL
QUESTIONS.

Strongly Agree	Agree	Neither Agree nor Disagree	Disagree	Strongly Disagree

1. I am allowed a high degree of influence in the
   determination of my work objectives.

   _____   _____   _____   _____   _____

2. I should not have too much difficulty in
   reaching my work objectives; they appear
   to be fairly easy.

   _____   _____   _____   _____   _____

3. I receive a considerable amount of feedback
   concerning my quantity of output on the job.

   _____   _____   _____   _____   _____

4. Most of my co-workers and peers try to
   outperform each other on their assigned
   sales quotas.

   _____   _____   _____   _____   _____

5. My work objectives are very clear and
   specific; I know exactly what my job is.

   _____   _____   _____   _____   _____

6. My work objectives will require a great deal of effort from me to complete them.

_____   _____   _____   _____   _____

7. I really have little voice in the formulation of my work objectives.

_____   _____   _____   _____   _____

Strongly Agree	Agree	Neither Agree nor Disagree	Disagree	Strongly Disagree

8. I am provided with a great deal of feedback and guidance on the quality of my work.

_____   _____   _____   _____   _____

9. I think my work objectives are ambiguous and unclear.

_____   _____   _____   _____   _____

10. It will take a high degree of skill and know-how on my part to attain fully my sales quota.

_____   _____   _____   _____   _____

11. The setting of my work is pretty much under my own control.

_____   _____   _____   _____   _____

12. My boss seldom lets me know how well I am doing toward my work objectives.

_____   _____   _____   _____   _____

13. There is a very competitive atmosphere among my peers and I with regard to attaining our respective sales quotas; we all want to do better in attaining our goals than anyone else.

_____   _____   _____   _____   _____

14. I understand fully which of my work objectives are more important than others; I have a clear sense of priorities on these goals.

_____   _____   _____   _____   _____

15. My work objectives are quite difficult to attain.

_____   _____   _____   _____   _____

YOU HAVE FINISHED THIS SECTION. PLEASE GO ON TO THE NEXT SECTION.

Table 13. Biographical Information

```
DIRECTIONS: In this section, you will be asked for
biographical information. Please place check marks
and fill in the blanks where appropriate.



    1.  What is your sex?     _____Male     _____Female


    2.  How old are you? (rounded to the nearest year)
        _____ years.


    3.  Please place a check mark beside the category
        which best describes your marital status.
        _____Separated
        _____Single
        _____Married
        _____Divorced


    4.  How many dependents do you have?  (Please EXCLUDE
        yourself.)
        I have _____ dependents.


    5.  Please place a check mark beside the category which
        best describes your educational background.
        _____ High school
        _____ Some college
        _____ College graduate
        _____ Some post-graduate education
        _____ Post-graduate degree


    6.  If you have attended some college, please check the
        category below which best describes the COURSE
        AREA which you concentrated in.
        _____ Technical
        _____ Business
        _____ Technical and Business
        _____ Other



    7.  The items below relate to your JOB EXPERIENCE.  Please
        write in the number which describes your situation
        for each of the three items.

           a.  Time in present or similar sales jobs _____years.
           b.  Time with this company _____years.
           c.  Time with your present product line _____years.

YOU HAVE FINISHED THE SECTION ON BIOGRAPHICAL INFORMATION.
PLEASE GO ON TO THE NEXT SECTION.
```

Table 14. A Subjective Performance Assessment

DIRECTIONS: In this section, you will be asked to SUBJECTIVELY compare the OVERALL JOB PERFORMANCE of EACH SALESPERSON in your district. Please take into account all factors which you feel are relevant to this assessment, including differing salesperson age, job experience, sales quotas, territory sales potential and other similar factors.

In order to assist you in this activity, a RATING SCALE and space to write the NAMES of the salespersons are provided on the next page.

Rate the BEST PERFORMING salesperson in your district as a "100" and place his (her) name beside the TOP "hash mark" given on the scale. (Please look at this scale now.)

Next, place the name of the POOREST PERFORMING salesperson by the BOTTOM "hash mark".

For ALL OTHER salespersons whose job performance is in between "best" and "worst", rate each person's job performance by placing a "tick mark" in a place on the scale which you feel represents his job performance relative to the job performance of everyone else, and write his name beside this "tick mark".

PLEASE GO ON TO THE NEXT PAGE AND RATE ALL OF THE SALESPERSONS IN YOUR DISTRICT ON JOB PERFORMANCE IN THE FASHION DESCRIBED ABOVE.

A Rating Scale for the Sales Manager to Rate the Job Performance of All of the Salespersons in His (Her) District

RATING SCALE	SALESPERSON NAMES
Top 10% ____	
90	
80% ____	

```
              70% ____

              60% ____

Average       50% ____

              40% ____

              30% ____

              20% ____

              10% ____
Bottom 10%
                  ____
```

BEFORE PROCEEDING PLEASE CHECK TO MAKE SURE YOU HAVE
RATED ALL OF YOUR SALESPERSONS. THANK YOU.
WHEN YOU HAVE FINISHED THE RATING OF THE SALESPERSONS
IN YOUR DISTRICT, PLEASE GO ON TO THE NEXT SECTION.

Table 15. An Objective Performance Assessment

An Objective Comparative Assessment Made by the Sales Manager of the Job Performance of Each Salesperson in His District Relative to the SALES QUOTA of Each

DIRECTIONS: In this section, you will be asked to give an OBJECTIVE assessment of each salesperson in your district with respect to his (her) JOB PERFORMANCE VS. SALES QUOTA for the calendar year 1979. Please just rate each salesperson's performance by stating what PERCENTAGE OF SALES QUOTA he attained in 1979.

In order to assist you in this activity, a RATING SCALE and space to write the NAMES of the salespersons are provided on the next page.

Rate the BEST PERFORMING salesperson in your district as a "100" and place his (her) name beside the TOP "hash mark" given on the scale. (Please look at this scale now.)

Next, place the name of the POOREST PERFORMING salesperson by the BOTTOM "hash mark".

For ALL OTHER salespersons whose job performance is in between "best" and "worst", rate each person's job performance by placing a "tick mark" in a place on the scale which you feel represents his job performance relative to the job performance of everyone else, and write his name beside this "tick mark".

PLEASE GO ON TO THE NEXT PAGE AND RATE ALL OF THE SALESPERSONS IN YOUR DISTRICT ON JOB PERFORMANCE IN THE FASHION DESCRIBED ABOVE.

A Rating Scale for the Sales Manager to Rate the Job Performance of All of the Salespersons in His (Her) District

RATING SCALE   SALESPERSON NAMES

Top 10%   ____

90

```
                    80% ____

                    70% ____

                    60% ____

     Average        50% ____

                    40% ____

                    30% ____

                    20% ____

                    10% ____
Bottom 10%
                        ____
```

BEFORE PROCEEDING PLEASE CHECK TO MAKE SURE YOU HAVE
RATED ALL OF YOUR SALESPERSONS. THANK YOU.
WHEN YOU HAVE FINISHED THE RATING OF THE SALESPERSONS
IN YOUR DISTRICT, PLEASE GO ON TO THE NEXT SECTION.

Table 16. Sales Volume Generated by Each Salesperson

DIRECTIONS: In this section, you will only be asked to state the DOLLAR SALES VOLUME which each salesperson in your district attained in the calendar year 1979.

For example, if John Doe's sales volume for 1979, then you would put:

SALESPERSON	SALES VOLUME
_____John Doe_____	__$780,000__

Please put the name and sales volume for 1979 for EACH salesperson in your district in the space provided below.

SALESPERSON	SALES VOLUME
_____	_____
_____	_____
_____	_____
_____	_____
_____	_____
_____	_____
_____	_____
_____	_____
_____	_____

WHEN YOU HAVE FINISHED THIS SECTION, PLEASE GO ON TO THE NEXT PAGE.

Table 17. End of Questionnaire

```
YOU HAVE COME TO THE END OF THIS QUESTIONNAIRE.  PLEASE
CHECK OVER THE QUESTIONNAIRE TO MAKE SURE THAT YOU
HAVE ANSWERED EVERYTHING.  (IF THERE ARE MISSING ITEMS
IN A QUESTIONNAIRE, IT MIGHT HAVE TO BE DISCARDED.)


WHEN YOU HAVE FINISHED DOING THE ABOVE, PLEASE PUT
THIS QUESTIONNAIRE INTO THE ENVELOPE PROVIDED FOR YOU
AND PLACE IT IN THE MAIL.  THANK YOU VERY MUCH FOR
YOUR TIME.  HOPEFULLY, YOU HAVE ENJOYED THINKING
ABOUT THE ISSUES THAT THIS QUESTIONNAIRE RAISES.




                         Nick Williamson
                         Project Director
                         Graduate School of Bus. Adm.
                         UNC - Chapel Hill
                         Chapel Hill, NC   27514
```

4

Results

4.1 Introduction

The purpose of this study is fourfold. First, the job performance predictive capabilities of a salesperson's valence for achieving personal sales goals is compared with the predictive capability of the salesperson's valence for attaining company goals (such as quotas). Secondly, an analysis is conducted which investigates whether or not "need Achievement" moderates the relationship between the scope of a sales job and sales performance.

Third, an enquiry is made concerning whether or not "need Achievement" moderates the effects of "task-goal attributes" on sales performance. Finally, an assessment is made as to whether or not "need Achievement" moderates the relationship between a salesperson's perceived probability (expectancy) of achieving his personal sales goal and job performance. This chapter presents the results and discussion of the regression models used to examine these interrelationships.

Initially, intercorrelational matrices of the constructs referred to in Figure 1 are presented. Correlations of particular interest are discussed, and statements concerning multicollinearity of the variables in the different variable sets are given. Second, regression models expressing the interrelationships among the variables assessed in the four hypotheses are given. In the next chapter are a discussion of the implications for salesperson motivation and performance of the results reported in this chapter and a description of a new model for predicting sales performance.

4.2 Correlations Among the Constructs Used

In Table 18 are given the intercorrelations among the two performance variables, the two "need Achievement" constructs, the Motivational Potential Score (MPS) variable and the "participation in quota-setting" variable. Given below is a commentary on how the correlations in Table 18 shed interesting and relevant light on the hypotheses stated.

Table 18. Overall Correlations among the Constructs

Variable name	V1	V2	V3	V4	V5	V6	V7
(1) Objective Performance	1.00						
(2) Subjective Performance	.78(d)	1.00					
(3) "n Ach"-MNQ	.35(c)	.33(c)	1.00				
(4) "n Ach"-Jackson	.12	.09	.46(d)	1.00			
(5) Valence for Co. goal	.10	.12	.11	.13	1.00		
(6) MPS	.13	.23(a)	.23(a)	.15	.44(d)	1.00	
(7) Participation in goal sett.	.11	.10	.24(a)	.09	.40(d)	.64(d)	1.00

Key: a = sig. at .05
      b = sig. at .01
      c = sig. at .001
      d = sig. at .0001

4.2.1 The Relationships among the "n Ach" Scales and Performance

Significant correlations between the subjective and objective performance variables and the "n Ach" scale in the Manifest Needs Questionnaire were uncovered (r = .35, p<.0009 for the objective performance measure and r = .33, p<.002 for the subjective measure). No significant correlation was found between the need Achievement scale developed by Jackson (1967) and either of the performance variables. Possible reasons for this lack of a correlation may stem from the fact that the Jackson "n Ach" scale is an "affective" scale, and sales performance is the outcome of a "behavior". Steers' scale for Need Achievement, however, is a "behavioral" scale, and past studies have shown that behavioral scales are more effective in predicting behaviorally-based variables than are affective scales. In addition, while Steers' scale was developed specifically to measure achievement motivation in work environments, the Jackson scale was not developed with this kind of specific focus.

Though a positive correlation between "need Achievement" and job performance was not originally hypothesized, a related precedent for this result can be found in the work of Doyle and Shapiro (1980). These researchers found that a significant relationship existed between a salesperson's need to achieve and the effort which the salesperson expends on the job.

4.2.2 The MPS Score and the Performance Variables

The zero order correlation between the Motivational Potential Score (MPS) and the subjective performance variable is significant ($r = .23$, $p<.04$). However, as will be shown later in this chapter, when the effects of a salesperson's need for achievement are controlled for, the first order correlation between the MPS score and the subjective performance variable become non-significant.

4.2.3 MPS and the Valence for Achieving the Company Goal

The perceived degree of enrichment of job (represented by the MPS score) is significantly associated with virtually all of the valence for performance composites, both adjusted for the standard deviation and unadjusted. (Due to space considerations, in Table 18 only the "valence for attaining the company goal" was shown. A more complete display of the valence composites will be shown in a later table.) The high correlation between the MPS variable and the valence for attaining the company goal could possibly be attributed to the incapability of the salespeople in the sample to conceptually discriminate between the different aspects of the design of the job and the extent to which performing well on the job leads to the reception of job outcomes.

4.2.4 The Performance Variables and the VIE Constructs

Three observations stem directly from an assessment of the correlations among the performance variables and the various hypothesized VIE consructs. (Table 19 gives the details of these zero order correlations).

1. The use of the salesman's personal goal as the focus of the expectancy and instrumentality variables did not provide a clearer relationship with the performance variables than did the relationship of the company qoal with the performance variables.

2. Regardless of whether the company goal or the personal goal is used as the focus of the IV construct, no significant correlation between any valence for performance construct and performance variable is found.

3. The adjustment of the valence for job outcomes variables and the instrumentality constructs by their respective standard deviations which each individual demonstrates in answering each of these sets of variables was not found to be useful in increasing the performance-predictive capabilities of the VIE-based model.

Table 19. Correlations among the Performance and VIE Constructs

	V1	V2	V3	V4	V5	V6	V7
Variable Names							
Subjective Perform.	1.00						
Objective Perform.	.78(d)	1.00					
Val. for Co. goal	.12	.10	1.00				
Val. for Pers. goal	.18	.13	.92(d)	1.00			
Adj. val for Co. goal	.01	.01	.62(d)	.57(d)	1.00		
Adj. val for Pers. goal	-.02	-.06	.54(d)	.55(d)	.90(d)	1.00	
Expectancy X Sum of IV	.19	.18	.90(d)	.86(d)	.61(d)	.54(d)	1.00

Key: a = sig. at .05 level
      b = sig. at .01 level
      c = sig. at .001 level
      d = sig. at .0001 level

For comparison, a correlation matrix among the same variables as are in the previous matrix is presented in Table 20, with the exception that the Σ (I × V) composite is computed on all 17 job outcomes and instrumentalities probed in the questionnaire rather than just the five most important job outcomes. A more complete description concerning why the above pattern of relationships evolved will be given in the discussion of the results of Hypothesis One later in this chapter.

4.2.5 Participation in Quota-Setting and Perceived Job Autonomy

Some question was brought up in Chapter 1 as to the nature of the effects that "participation in quota-setting" might have on job performance. Some persons might view the participation process as a "whip" (Raia, 1969) which the sales supervisor could use to hold the salesperson excessively accountable for the outcome of his short-term sales performance. If this were the case, then presumably, this "participatory" process would affect the salesperson's perceptions of his autonomy on the job.

Table 20. Correlation Matrix Using All Seventeen Job Outcomes

Variable name	V1	V2	V3	V4	V5	V6	V7
Subjective Performance	1.00						
Objective Performance	0.79d	1.00					
Valence for Ach. co. g.	0.13	0.12	1.00				
Valence for Ach. pers. g.	0.15	0.09	0.93d	1.00			
Adjusted Val. for Ach.c.g.	0.02	0.03	0.71d	0.73d	1.00		
Adjusted V. for Ach pers. g.	0.00	-.03	0.63d	0.70d	0.90d	1.00	
Expectancy X Sum(I x V)	0.07	0.08	0.68d	0.69d	0.97d	0.87d	1.00

When one correlates the participation variable in Table 18 and the autonomy variable, which is a component variable of the MPS score, a significant relationship is brought to light ($r = .78$, $p < .0001$). Furthermore, the nature of this correlation does not depend upon the need for achievement of the salesperson. When "need Achievement" is used as a two level factor, and when one tests the homogeneity of regression slopes between the participation variable and the autonomy variable, these slopes are virtually identical ($F = 0.00$, $p < .99$). In sum, salespeople in the sample assessed do not view the participatory process in forming company goals (quotas) as an infringement upon their sense of autonomy on the job. That is, these salespeople do not view the participatory process as a "whip" to use on them.

4.2.6 Intercorrelations among the Predictor Variables

An assessment of the intercorrelations among the VIE variables given in Table 19 and the MPS and MBO variables given in Table 21 below, together with the overall correlations given in Table 18 indicate that there are substantial intercorrelations among different predictor variables in different predictor sets.

The high correlations among the variables of a given predictor set, such as the MPS variables, is expected. Each of these variables purports to explain different aspects of the characteristics of a sales job which refer to the "scope" or "enrichment" of the job. A similar line of reasoning applies to the MBO variables, dealing in different "task-goal attributes".

Again, high correlations between two different variables which come from different predictor sets—such as the correlation between goal-specificity and task significance ($r = .35$, $p < .0008$)—indicate that the salespeople in the sample may not view the job enrichment and task-goal attribute variables as distinct entities. The same line of reasoning appears to apply when one assesses the high correlation ($r = .44$, $p < .0001$) between the MPS score and the valence for achieving the company goal.

Table 21. Correlations among the MPS and MBO Variables

Variable Name	V1	V2	V3	V4	V5	V6	V7	V8	V9	V10
Variety	1.0									
Task Identity	.21a	1.0								
Task Signif.	.45d	.22a	1.0							
Autonomy	.24a	.34c	.30c	1.0						
Feedback	.43d	.51d	.44d	.20	1.0					
Participation	.24a	.33c	.24a	.78d	.26a	1.0				
Goal Difficulty	.31b	-.01	.31b	-.07	.16	-.14	1.0			
Feedbac2	.23a	.39c	.17	.18	.32b	.19	.02	1.0		
Peer Compet.	.03	.00	.14	-.07	.13	.01	.05	.21a	1.0	
Goal Specific.	.12	.42d	.35c	.42d	.36c	.53d	-.08	.38c	.14	1.0

Key: a = sig. at the .05 level
      b = sig. at the .01 level
      c = sig. at the .001 level
      d = sig. at the .0001 level

4.3 Scale Analysis

This section concerns the analysis of the job scope variables, the task-goal attribute variables and the two "need Achievement" scales. The Cronbach Alpha coefficient is the test used to determine whether or not the scales performed with sufficient reliability. Table 22 below gives the results of the analyses. The scales appeared to perform adequately.

Table 22. Test of the Reliability of the Scales Used

VARIABLE	ALPHA
Task-goal attributes	
1. Participation	.62
2. Goal difficulty	.70
3. Feedback (second scale)	.77
4. Peer competition	.73
5. Goal specificity	.69
"need Achievement" scales	
1. Jackson	.59
2. MNQ	.51
Job scope variables	
1. Variety	.66
2. Task identity	.63
3. Task significance	.76
4. Autonomy	.76
5. Feedback (first scale)	.73

4.4 Qualification of the Performance Variables

Of the four performance variables which were originally intended to be used in this study, only the objective and the subjective performance estimates were deemed to be acceptable for use. The "Sales" performance variable and the "Adjusted sales" performance variable were not acceptable, as is described below.

4.4.1 The Sales Variable

After the data were gathered, it was determined that many of the subjects from Companies I and II who participated in the study performed missionary activities, or were national accounts salespeople, part revenue-generating salesperson. Thus, the "sales" figure rendered can give a distorted view of the actual performance of the salesperson.

92 Results

4.4.2 The Adjusted Sales Variable

Of the four variables used to "adjust" the sales figures for bias, two variables—"territory potential" and "time in product line"—were answered in different ways by different salespeople. For territory potential, many salespeople put down exact (to the penny) dollar figures, which indicated that they thought that "territory potential" and revenues which had already been generated were the same thing.

For "time in product line", some salespeople used the term "product line" in the broadest sense—that is, how long they had handled the generic product. For others, however, "time in product line" referred to the time the salesperson sold the product line while working for the company.

4.4.3 The Objective Performance Variable

As was described earlier, the performance variable was constructed so as to overcome problems such as (1) the long lead time between salesperson efforts and realized sales and (2) the notion that issues such as differing salesperson experience bases, geographical territory sizes, spans of control of the salesperson's supervisor and differing territory sales potentials can significantly affect sales performance (Ryans and Weinberg, 1979). Table 22A reports the intercorrelations among the "sales" variable, the objective performance variable, and the four variables alluded to above.

Since the denomination of "sales" was different for each company, the Pearson Product-Moment Correlation Matrix given in Table 22A was formed by standardizing each of the six variables for the sample within each company and then pooling the results "across companies" for correlations. As one might expect, the correlation between the objective performance variable and "sales" is significant ($r = .30$, $p<.01$).

Also, there is a significant correlation between the objective performance variable and the territory sales potential variable ($r = .32$, $p<.01$). There is, correspondingly, a positive correlation between the "sales" variable and the territory potential variable. The positive correlation between the objective performance variable and the territory potential variable probably is largely due to the policy of Company I of rewarding good performers by giving them sales territories having larger than average sales potentials.

It is important to note in Table 22A, the fact that the correlation between the objective performance variable and the sales variable (.30) is less than the correlation between the objective performance variable and the territory potential variable (.32). This is possible evidence that the objective performance variable lacks construct validity. Also, the low correlation between the objective performance variable and the sales variable could be due to a "suppressor" effect from one of the remaining four variables in Table 5.

Table 22A. Pearson Product-Moment Correlation Matrix for the Objective Performance Variable, the "Sales" Variable and Four Variables Which May Bias the Objective Performance and "Sales" Variables

	OP1	S1	SQM1	SP1	EXP1	TP1
Objective Performance	1.00	.30[b]	.02	.13	.08	.32[b]
Sales		1.00	-.09	.00	.31[b]	.23[a]
Square Miles			1.00	.08	-.06	-.13
Span				1.00	.02	.09
Sales Experience					1.00	.01
Territory Potential						1.00

"a" denotes significance at the .05 level
"b" denotes significance at the .01 level

There is a systematic positive correlation between the "sales" variable and the salesperson's length of time selling his(her) product line with the company (r = .31, p<.01). However, no relationship exists between the objective performance variable and the salesperson's experience with selling the product line. Thus, with the exception of the correlation with "territory sales potential," the objective performance variable in this study exhibits the desired properties. It is significantly correlated with "sales", and, yet, this variable is not confounded by the salesperson's experience variable.

4.5 Results of the Tests of the Four Hypotheses

The four hypotheses which this research is structured to investigate are listed below to provide a focus for the balance of this chapter.

> Hypothesis One: A salesperson's valence for achieving quota and valence for achieving personal sales goal are positively related with sales performance. Furthermore, the valence for achieving one's personal sales goal is a better predictor of sales performance than is the valence for achieving one's company goal. Finally, adjusting the individual valence for job outcomes and instrumentalities of achieving sales goal variables by the standard deviation which each salesperson exhibits in answering the complete sets of valence for job outcomes and instrumentality variables will allow one a greater performance predictive capability than is available without the adjustment.

Hypothesis Two: When the valence for achieving sales quota and the valence for achieving one's personal sales goal are used as covariates, "need Achievement" moderates the relationship between Job Scope (job enrichment) and sales performance.

Hypothesis Three: "Need Achievement" moderates the relationship between "participation in quota-setting" and sales performance when the valence for sales quota and the valence for attaining personal sales goal are used as covariates.

Hypothesis Four: When "expectancy" is defined as one's own personal sales goal, and when the valence for attaining one's own sales goal is used as a covariate, "need Achievement" moderates the relationship between "expectancy" and sales performance.

Before going into the specific results which shed light on the validity of the hypotheses, note must be made concerning differing mean characteristics between the sample of salespersons used in this study and the sample of managers and professional people whom Steers and Braunstein (1976) used in the development of the "need Achievement" scale of the Manifest Needs Questionnaire. On the whole, the salespersons used in this study had a significantly greater mean need for achievement than did the members of the sample used by Steers and Braunstein. Whereas, the mean "n Ach" score of the present sample was 7.29 with a standard error of the mean being 0.31, the mean "need Achievement" score calculated for the Steers and Braunstein sample was 4.2 with a standard error of the mean of 0.75. Thus, one may conservatively infer that these two samples of respondents differ on their mean need to achieve at the .01 level of significance.

With the populations differing to this extent on a construct (need Achievement) which has been the mainspring for the development of the hypotheses tested in this study, one may not correctly state that the results of this study shed disconfirming (or confirming) light on the validity of the studies of Steers (Steers and Spencer, 1977; Steers, 1975; Steers, 1976). These studies did not use salespersons as the sample frame, and salespersons apparently constitute, as a body, a group of individuals very high in the need to achieve.

By way of comparison, a great majority of the persons in this study who are classified in this study as being low in "n Ach" would be classified as high in need Achievement in the studies conducted by Steers. Only 17 of the 44 persons who are classified as being low in need Achievement in this study would also be classified as low in "n Ach" using the standards developed by Steers and Braunstein.

It is only fair to say, then, that the results of analyses reported in this study are more exploratory in their implications for salesforce research than they are confirming or disconfirming to the theories developed by Steers, which ostensibly apply to persons working in a broader range of positions in organizations. In order to attempt to see if the four hypotheses tested are confirmable not only within the sample frame tested but also outside of this sample frame, an additional set of analyses will be reported for Hypotheses Two and Three in which the salespersons are divided into high and low need achievers, using the criterion of Steers and Braunstein (1976). That is, the 17 persons scoring 4 or less on the MNQ need for achievement scale are assigned to one group low in ("n Ach") and the other 72 persons will be assigned to another group high in the ("n Ach"). (Note: Due to the instability of the results which may stem from this lopsided division, the results should be interpreted with caution.)

Before the results of the tests of the hypotheses are given, a final note should be made concerning the relationship between the MNQ "need Achievement" scale and the objective and subjective performance variables. As was noted earlier, these relationships are significant ($r = .35$, $p<.001$ for the objective performance variable, and $r = .33$, $p<.002$ for the subjective performance variable). This situation did not occur in Steers and Spencer (1977) and Steers (1976).

In order to account for this situation, and in order to reflect the fact that the "valence for attaining one's personal sales goal" and the "valence for attaining the company goal" are significantly related with either of the performance variables, the MNQ "need Achievement" variable will be used in addition to the valence composite variables as a covariate. Also included in the analyses for Hypotheses Two, Three and Four are tables in which the valence composites are based on the entire set of 17 job outcomes and instrumentalities rather than just the 5 most important outcomes and instrumentalities.

4.6 Empirical Tests of the Four Hypotheses

In this section are reported the results of the empirical tests of the four hypotheses which this research addresses. For each hypothesis, there will first be a statement of the hypothesis. Following this statement will be tables which summarize the empirical results of the analyses conducted.

There will be two sets of analyses for Hypotheses Two and Three. For each of these two hypotheses, the first set of analyses will reflect the division of the sample into two approximately equal halves, based upon the MNQ "n Ach" scale scores. The second set of analyses for Hypotheses Two and Three will reflect the results of these hypotheses using the norms of Steers and Braunstein (1976) for persons high in "n Ach" and persons low in "n Ach".

> Hypothesis One: A salesperson's valence for achieving quota and valence for achieving personal sales goal are positively related with sales performance. Furthermore, the valence for achieving one's personal sales goal is a better predictor of sales performance than is the valence for achieving one's company goal. Finally, adjusting the individual valence for job outcomes and instrumen-

Results

Table 23. Hypothesis One Regressions

REGRESSIONS TESTING THE VALIDITY OF HYPOTHESIS ONE WHEN THE SUBJECTIVE PERFORMANCE MEASURE IS THE DEPENDENT VAR.

Independent	Estimate	Std. err. of est.	F value	p <
Valence for att. co. g.	.905	.808	1.25	0.27
Valence for att per. g.	1.311	.790	2.75	0.10
Adjusted Valence for att. co. g.	.007	.071	0.01	0.92
Adjusted Valence for att. per. g.	-.011	.061	0.04	0.85

REGRESSIONS TESTING THE VALIDITY OF HYPOTHESIS ONE WHEN THE OBJECTIVE PERFORMANCE MEASURE IS THE DEPENDENT VAR.

Predictor	Estimate	Std. err	F Value	p <
Valence for att. co. g.	0.682	0.712	0.92	0.34
Valence for att. per. g.	0.881	0.700	1.58	0.21
Adjusted Valence for att. co. g.	0.007	0.063	0.01	0.91
Adjusted Valence for att. per. g.	-.03	0.053	0.32	0.58

talities of achieving sales goal variables by the standard deviation which each salesperson exhibits in answering the complete sets of valence for job outcomes and instrumentality variables will allow one a greater performance predictive capability than is available without the adjustment.

The results of the test of this hypothesis are disconfirming and yield the same information as was gathered from the correlation matrix in Table 18 alluded to previously. The results concerning these univariate regressions are given in Table 23 and can be summarized as follows:

1. Neither the valence for achieving one's company sales goal nor the valence for achieving one's personal sales goal is correlated with either the subjective performance measure or the objective performance measure.

2. The adjustment of the "5 most important" job outcomes and their corresponding instrumentalities by dividing these entities by the standard deviations exhibited by each respondent in answering the whole set of 17 individual instrumentalities and valences did not increase the performance predictive capabilities of the valence for performance composites.

Table 24. Hypothesis One Regressions Using All Seventeen Job Outcomes

For the Subjective Performance Measure

Indep. Var.	Estimate	Std. Err.	F Value	p <
Valence for att.co.g.	-0.28	1.02	0.08	0.78
Valence for att. per.g.	1.21	1.11	1.20	0.27
Adj v. for att.co.g.	0.01	0.07	0.03	0.85
Adj v. for att.per.g.	-.05	0.06	0.86	0.35

(The figures are not appreciably different for the objective performance measure.)

Given in Table 24 are similar figures using all 17 of the job outcomes. Result 1 above indicates that, for the sample frame of salespersons used, neither the "valence for attaining the company goal" nor the "valence for attaining the personal goal" was significantly correlated with either of the two performance measures with the probability of a Type I error set at the .05 level. There are several reasons why there may not have been a significant correlation. One reason is that the individual valence for job outcomes variables and their respective instrumentality variables are significantly correlated in many instances. This correlation may be indicative of a lack of discriminating ability on the part of the members of the sample to distinguish between the individual valence and instrumentality variables.

In Table 25 are given the correlations among the valences for the first five job outcomes and their respective instrumentalities. For 3 of the 5 variables, the valence variables are correlated with their respective instrumentality variables at the .01 level. The proper predictive performance of either the valence for achieving one's company goal or the valence for achieving the personal goal requires that the valence for outcome and instrumentality variables fluctuate independently of each other.

Another possible reason for the lack of a significant correlation between either of the two composite valence scores and the performance variables stems from the homogeneity of the responses on the valence for job outcomes variables. The Likert-type scale used to score the valence for job outcomes variables had a range of -2 (very undesirable) to $+2$ (very desirable). However, a majority of the responses on many of the outcome variables were answered "$+2$" by the respondents. Thus, variation in the evidence for performance composites appears to be largely caused by variation in the instrumentality variables which go into the composite, and the valence for job outcomes variables are largely factored out of the composite.

Table 25. Correlations among the Valences and Outcomes

	Instrument. for co.g.1	Instrument. for co.g.2	Instrument. for co.g.3	Instrument. for co.g.4	Instrument. for co.g.
Outc. 1	0.10 (0.36)	0.09 (0.41)	0.13 (0.21)	0.09 (0.37)	0.10 (0.36)
Outc. 2	0.28 (0.007)	0.46 (0.0001)	0.17 (0.11)	0.12 (0.27)	0.13 (0.22)
Outc. 3	0.04 (0.69)	0.19 (0.07)	0.31 (0.003)	0.01 (0.91)	0.06 (0.59)
Outc. 4	0.12 (0.26)	0.20 (0.06)	0.23 (0.02)	0.36 (0.0004)	0.35 (0.0008)
Outc. 5	0.16 (0.12)	0.13 (0.21)	0.20 (0.05)	0.14 (0.17)	0.17 (0.10)

Note: The upper figures refer to the zero order correlations, a the lower figures are the $p <$ figures.

4.6.0.1 The adjustment of the V and I vars. by their std. devs. The division by their respective standard deviations of the individual valence for job outcome variables and their respective instrumentality variables which make up the $\Sigma(I \times V)$ composite for each valence composite did not increase the performance predicting capability of the composite. The reverse situation appeared to be the case.

Though there is no certainty why this adjustment failed, the adjustment itself intended to give greater weight to those respondents who exhibited smaller standard deviations in their responses to the valence for job outcomes and instrumentality sets. The reasoning behind this effect can be noted from an inspection of the way that the adjustment affects the valence for performance composite. This formula is given in Table 26 below.

The (σ_I) and (σ_v) figures are constants for each respondent and represent scalars which adjust the $\Sigma(I \times V)$ composite which is the typical formulation for a "valence for performance" composite. Please note that as either (σ_I) for (σ_v) become smaller, the overall effect is to increase the magnitude of the adjusted composite. Correspondingly, having larger standard deviations decreases the size of the adjusted composite. Apparently, the benefits which this adjustment affords the researcher in making the responses homogeneous with respect to their standard deviations on the valence and instrumentality variables was outweighed by the fact that a substantial number of persons exhibited little variation in the valence and instrumentality categories. As a result, their adjusted valence for performance composites balooned in a more than linear fashion.

Table 26. Formula for Adjusting the Valence Composite

$$(I/\sigma_I) \times (V/\sigma_v) = (1/(\sigma_I) \times (\sigma_v)) \times (\Sigma I \times V)$$

4.6.0.2 Discussion of the results of the Hypothesis One analyses The results of the analyses incident to the test of Hypothesis One give more indications that a process model based upon a linear combination of Vroomian valence and instrumentality constructs is not useful for predicting a person's performance in an organization. Perhaps the most fundamental shortcoming uncovered in looking at the results of Hypotheses One analyses concerns the high correlations of the individual valence for job outcomes variables with their respective instrumentality variables. This lack of independence invalidates the viability of the linear model at a fundamental level: whether or not this is due to a measurement problem concerning the specific instrument used or a problem with the theory, the salespeople in the sample were unable to conceptually separate the valence for a given job outcome and the instrumentality which achieving a performance goal has for receiving that job outcome. When one adds to this the notion that the individual valence for job outcome variables are essentially factored out of the $\Sigma(I \times V)$ composite due to the restriction of range which characterizes the responses on

Table 27. The Motivational Potential Score and Performance

RESULTS OF THE REGRESSIONS OF THE MOTIVATING POTENTIAL
SCORE ON THE SUBJECTIVE AND OBJECTIVE PERFORMANCE VARS.

For the Subjective
Performance var.:

Variable	F Value	$p <$
"n Ach"	4.41	0.03
Valence for att.co.goal	1.32	0.25
Valence for att.per.g.	1.81	0.18
MPS	1.14	0.28
MPS X "n Ach" Interaction	0.01	0.92

For the Objective
Performance var.:

Variable	F Value	$p <$
"n Ach"	2.14	0.14
Valence for att.co.goal	0.38	0.54
Valence for att.per.goal	0.91	0.34
MPS	0.03	0.86
MPS X "n Ach" interaction	1.38	0.24

these variables, then the Vroomian notion concerning the composite "valence for performance" is transformed into a construct concerning the "instrumentality of performance".

Possibly a more fruitful path to follow would be to determine which of the 17 individual job outcomes are typically preferred by high performing salespeople and which other job outcomes are preferred by low performing salespeople. In doing this, one would no longer have a process theory of motivation based upon a composite known at the "valence for performance". One would have a content theory of motivation based upon the valence for individual job outcomes.

Whereas, the instrumentalities of performance and the valences for job outcomes form the basis for the VIE-based theories of motivation, the degree of enrichment or the "scope" of a job represents another dimension which possibly has implications for the motivation of salespersons on the job. This is the topic of Hypothesis Two, and the results of the analyses testing the validity of Hypothesis Two are given in the next section.

4.6.1 The Effects of Job Scope on Sales Performance

Hypothesis Two: "Need Achievement" moderates the relationship between Job Scope and Sales Performance.

In the discussion concerning the correlations among the major sets of variables in this study, given in Table 18, note was made of a significant zero order correlation which existed between the MPS variable (which is an overall measure of the degree of enrichment or scope of a job) and the subjective performance variable ($r = .23$, $p < .04$). When the effects of "need Achievement" are controlled for, the correlation between the MPS construct and the subjective performance measure becomes non-significant ($F(1,86) = 0.30$, $p < .59$). The results of these regressions are shown in Table 27.

The results given in Table 27 show that the MPS score is in no way significantly related with either performance variable, either moderated or otherwise.

Given in Table 28 and Table 29 are the results of the same analyses, only using the "n Ach" norm of Steers in Table 28 and including all 17 job outcomes in the calculation of the valence composites in Table 29. (Note: no single variable or combination of variables which go into the MPS score is significantly correlated with either performance variable when "n Ach" is used as a covariate.)

Table 28. Hypothesis Two using Steers' Norms

Dependent Var.	Independent Var.	F Value	p <
Subjective Performance	n Ach	1.76	0.18
	MPS	2.68	0.10
	MPS X n Ach	0.28	0.60
Objective Performance	n Ach	0.63	0.43
	MPS	0.24	0.62
	MPS X n Ach	0.02	0.88

Table 29. MPS with the Expanded (I × V)

Dependent var.	Independent Var.	F Value	p <
Subjective Performance	n Ach	5.07	0.03
	Valence for Att. co. g.	0.00	0.97
	Valence for Att. per. g.	0.00	0.96
	MPS	1.72	0.19
	MPS X n Ach	0.16	0.69
Objective Performance	n ach	3.35	0.07
	Val. for Att. Co. goal	1.25	0.27
	Val. for Att. Personal goal	1.11	0.29
	MPS	0.03	0.86
	MPS X n Ach	0.46	0.50

4.6.1.1 Discussion of the results of Hypothesis Three analyses One possible reason for the negative results concerning the test of Hypothesis Two centers on the fact that the salespersons used in this study are relatively high in the need to achieve on the job. Restriction of range on the "n Ach" variable is thus a problem. Another possible reason for the pattern of results generated might be that the perceived degree of enrichment of a sales job is just not motivationally salient to the salesperson. Though no hard data presently exists to support this notion, it seems logical that when a salesperson takes a sales position within a company and stays in this position for a significant time period, the salesperson becomes aware of the limitations of the job. And if one assumes that not much can be done to "enrich" a sales job, the very fact that a salesperson stays with the job may indicate that the enrichment of a job is not a motivationally salient issue to him.

While the MPS score relates to the degree of enrichment of a job, other issues such as the participation with sales management in making the sales quota and the specificity of the sales quota are issues of potential motivational significance which relate to the attributes of the tasks and goals. These attributes and their performance predicting capabilities are the subject matter of Hypothesis Three. The results of the analyses related to Hypothesis Three are presented in the next section.

4.6.2 Results of the Analyses Related to Hypothesis Three

Hypothesis Three: "Need Achievement" moderates the relationship between participation in quota-setting and sales performance.

Again, please keep in mind the notion that the "n Ach" scale was added to the two valence composites as a covariate.

According to the work of Steers (1975), persons low in "n Ach" should be positively motivated to perform by participation in quota-setting, since this action would "ego-involve" these persons to a greater extent in their work. Persons high in need Achievement, however, would be unaffected by this participation process. Table 30 gives the results of the analysis of Hypothesis Three.

In Table 31 and Table 32 are the results of the same analyses as above. In Table 31, the need Achievement norm of Steers is used. And in Table 32, all 17 job outcomes are used in the calculation of the valence composites.

Table 30. Results of the Analysis of Hypothesis Three

Dependent Var.	Indep. Var.	F Value	p <
Subjective Performance	n Ach	9.37	0.003
	Valence for Att. co. g.	1.03	0.31
	Valence for Att. per. g.	2.17	0.14
	Particip.	0.01	0.91
	Particip. X "n Ach"	0.16	0.69
Objective Performance	n Ach	7.80	0.007
	Valence for Att. co. g.	0.40	0.52
	Valence for Att. per. g.	0.94	0.33
	Particip.	0.11	0.74
	Particip. X "n Ach"	0.84	0.36

The results do not change when the norm for high and low "n Ach" persons reported by Steers and Braunstein is used for dividing the sample into persons high and low in the need to achieve. Also, the results do not change when one uses valence composites as covariates which use the entire set of 17 job outcomes rather than the five most important job outcomes.

Judging from the results reported in these tables, neither "participation in quota-setting" nor the "participation" × "n Ach" interaction explains variation in sales performance to any significant extent. One reason behind these disconfirming results, again, possibly lies in the fact that the sample of salespersons used in this study is, on the whole, very high in the need to achieve.

If one were to consider, for the moment, that the entire sample of salespersons was high in "n Ach", the results would not shed disconfirming light on Hypothesis Three. This is due to the fact that, in Steers (1975) study persons high in "n Ach" were supposed to be unaffected by the participatory process. Persons low in the need to achieve were the ones who benefited by this process.

Table 31. Results of Hypothesis Three using Steers' Norm

Dependent Var.	Independent Var.	F Value	p <
Subjective perf.	participation	1.07	0.30
	part X n Ach	0.90	0.34
	n Ach	5.80	0.02
Objective perf.	participation	0.36	0.55
	part X n Ach	0.07	0.79
	n Ach	5.55	0.02

4.6.2.1 Discussion of the results of Hypothesis Three Participation in the goal-setting process does not appear to be a motivationally salient issue for the salespersons used in this study. One interesting point lies in the fact that "participation" is so highly correlated with the MPS variable ($r = .64$, $p < .0001$). (For reference, please look at Table 18.) In light of this high correlation, one might rightfully wonder whether "participation" might be better classified as a job scope variable rather than a "task-goal" variable.

One construct which has not been addressed in any of the three hypotheses already addressed but which has been a center of controversy in many motivational circles is the "expectancy" construct, which refers to the salesperson's perceived probability of achieving production goals (both company and personal) in the future. "Expectancies" concerning company and personal goals and their possible impact on salesperson performance are topics addressed in the discussion of the results of analyses relevant to Hypothesis Four.

Table 32. Results of Hypothesis Three Using All Seventeen Job Outcomes

Dependent Variable	Independent Variable	F Value	p <
Subjective perf.	n Ach	8.94	0.004
	Valence for att. Co. goal	0.08	0.77
	Valence for att. personal goal	0.00	0.95
	participation	0.01	0.92
	participation X n Ach	0.51	0.47
Objective perf.	n Ach	8.85	0.004
	Valence for att. Co. goal	1.19	0.28
	Valence for att. personal goal	1.01	0.31
	participation	0.01	0.92
	participation X n Ach	0.12	0.73

4.6.3 Results of the Analyses Concerning Hypothesis Four

Hypothesis Four: When "expectancy" is defined as the "perceived probability of achieving one's own personal sales goal", "need Achievement" moderates the relationship between "expectancy" and sales performance.

As was alluded to in Chapters 1 and 2, there is some controversy as to the nature of the motivational impact of the "expectancies" which salespeople develop concerning the probability of success of their efforts to achieve company goals. The two lines of research which give support to the motivational importance of expectancies and which have distinct stances in this issue are the research work of Vroom (1964) and Locke, et al., (1970). Vroom's stance would be that a salesperson's expectancy of achieving his company goal would be positively related with sales performance. Locke, on the other hand, would state that the more difficult a company goal is—if the goal is accepted by the salesperson—the more motivating to the salesperson that the goal would be. This stance, then, would be in direct opposition to the stance of Vroom.

Results

Table 33 details the regression results concerning the relationship between the expectancy of achieving the company goals and the subjective and objective performance estimates.

Though a nearly significant correlation between the expectancy construct and the two performance measures is demonstrated ($p<.07$), the evidence is not sufficiently strong to lend support to either Locke or Vroom.

Table 33. Preliminary Hypothesis Four Regressions

REGRESSIONS CONCERNING THE RELATIONSHIPS BETWEEN THE EXPECTANCY OF ACHIEVING THE COMPANY GOAL AND THE TWO PERFORMANCE VARIABLES

Dependent Var.	Indep. Var.	Estimate	Std. Err.	F Value	p <
Subjective per.	Expectancy	25.80	14.32	3.25	0.07
Objective per.	Expectancy	22.77	12.58	3.27	0.07

A key issue in this area lies in the notion that a goal must be accepted by the salesperson if the company goal and the expectancy concerning its attainment are to be motivationally salient to the salesperson, regardless of the nature of the impact of expectancy. In order to insure that information concerning a goal which the salesperson accepts was available for this research, the respondents were asked to state their own personal production goals, and to give the perceived probability (expectancy) that they would achieve this personal goal.

The implementation of expectancy in reference to the personal goal allows one to test the theory of Atkinson. According to the theory of Atkinson, persons high in "need Achievement" seek personal goals in which the persons have a probability of success of approximately .5. Persons low in "n Ach", however, develop personal goals which are either very difficult (pr. of success = .1) or very easy (pr. of success = .9).

The most direct test of Hypothesis Four is the test of equivalence of the regression slopes between high "n Ach" persons and low "n Ach" persons for the relationship between sales performance and the expectancy of achieving one's own personal sales goal. The results of this test are given in Table 34.

Table 34 gives the results of Hypothesis Four. It is of interest to note that after the effects of the "need Achievement" variable and the variable relating to the expectancy of achieving one's own personal sales goal are eliminated, there is a significant relationship between the expectancy "need Achievement" interaction and the Objective Performance variable ($F = 4.01$, $p<.05$). That is, "need

Table 34. Test for a "Need Achievement"–Moderated Relationship Between the Expectancy of Achieving One's Own Personal Sales Goal and the Objective Performance Variable

Dependent Variable

OP

Source	DF	Type I SS	F Value	Pr < F
AM	1	2758.09	12.35	0.0007
EP	1	436.73	1.96	0.16
AM EP	1	894.43	4.01	0.04

ESTIMATE OF THE REGRESSION SLOPE for PERSONS SCORING ABOVE the SAMPLE AVERAGE on the "NEED ACHIEVEMENT" VARIABLE

Dependent Variable	Source	DF	Sums of Squares	Estimate	Pr > F
OP	EP	1.45	507.76	66.95	0.03

ESTIMATE of the REGRESSION SLOPE for PERSONS SCORING BELOW the SAMPLE AVERAGE on the "NEED ACHIEVEMENT" VARIABLE

Dependent Variable	Source	DF	Sums of Squares	Estimate	Pr > F
OP	EP	1.40	17.32	5.01	0.82

AM = Achievement Motivation
EP = Expectancy of Achieving One's Personal Sales Goal
OP = Objective Performance Variable

Achievement" moderates the relationship between a salesperson's expectancy of achieving his(her) own personal sales goal and the Objective Performance variable.

Furthermore, the bottom part of Table 34 indicates the nature of the moderated relationship. For those members in the sample who scored above the overall average sample score on the "need Achievement" variable, there is a positive relationship between "expectancy" the Objective Performance score ($F = 4.89$, $p<.05$). For those persons who score below the sample mean score on the "need Achievement" variable, there is no relationship between "expectancy" and "need Achievement" ($F = 0.05$, $p<.83$).

The results of the testing of Hypothesis Four are interesting in that one gains a fairly clear view into the motivational impact of the "expectancy" variable. For persons high in the need to achieve on the job, there appears to be a positive relationship between a salesperson's expectancy of achieving his(her) own personal sales goal and his job performance. No such relationship exists for persons low in the need to achieve on the job.

It is instructive to see how these results reflect on the motivational theories of Vroom (1964), Locke (1968) and Atkinson (1964). Vroom's theory, based upon the Law of Effect, receives partial support. That is, the expectancy construct functions in the fashion prescribed by Vroom for those persons high in the need to achieve on the job and when the focus of the expectancy calculation is the salesperson's personal sales goal.

Though the results provide definite disconfirmation of the goal-setting theory of Locke (1968), an assessment of the intercorrelations among the "need Achievement" variable and the two expectancy constructs shed some light as to how one might be led to find support for Locke's theory if the hierarchical regressions had not been conducted. There is nearly a positive correlation between "need Achievement" and the expectancy of achieving the company-generated performance targets ($r = .18$, $p<.08$). On the other hand, sketchy, though not significant, evidence exists that "need Achievement" and the expectancy of achieving the salesperson's own personal sales goal are negatively related ($r = -.12$, $p<.24$). That is, the greater the salesperson's need to achieve on the job, the more difficult the goals are that he(she) sets for himself. Latham and Yukl (1978) report the results of research where a significant negative relationship is found between the difficulty of the goal the employee sets and the employee's need to achieve. The key issue here is that the effects of the metric "need Achievement" variable—already shown to be an important predictor of sales performance—need to be partialled out of the expectancy/job performance relationship before a statement can be made concerning the independent influence of expectancy on job performance.

One cannot say with any degree of confidence that Atkinson's (1964) theory received disconfirmation. The reason can be found in an inspection of Equation 1. Atkinson gives an explicit position on the effects of expectancy on task (job) performance, but says that "extrinsic motivation" can also play a part in the calculation. One would imagine that "extrinsic motivation" (Churchill, Ford and Walker, 1976; Walker, Churchill and Ford, 1977) would play an important role in the sales environment, since a salesperson's pay level and, indeed, job security would depend upon goal accomplishment. Thus, Atkinson might argue that the effects of "extrinsic motivation" would "swamp" the effects of expectancy in this research.

Parallel events are reported in those studies researching the relationships among the self-esteem, job satisfaction and job performance variables (Korman, 1970; Jacobs and Solomon, 1977; Bagozzi, 1980). Korman (1970) states that a (sales)person acts in such a way to maximize his sense of cognitive balance or consistency with his own self-image. Korman states that there is a correlation between task success and satisfaction in persons who are high in self-esteem, and no correlation for persons low in self-esteem. Jacobs and Solomon (1977) report similar results, and Bagozzi (1980) establishes the nature of the causal sequence: self-esteem ▶ job performance ▶ job satisfaction.

The picture which emerges can be summarized as follows: only goal-oriented salespeople (i.e., salespeople who have a high need to achieve on the job and/or have high self-esteem) are motivationally affected by the expectancies which they develop concerning the attainment of their goals, and the motivational affect which is produced by these expectancies is in keeping with the Law of Effect (Vroom, 1964). The maximization of one's cognitive consistency rather than the cognitive consistency optimization implied by Atkinson (1964) or the minimization implied by Locke (1968) appears to be motivationally functional.

5

Summary, Implications and Suggestions for Further Research

In this chapter, a review of the findings is presented. Included in this review are both a summary of the major empirical findings relevant to the four hypotheses posited and a refined version of the conceptual model of the antecedents of salesperson motivation and performance.

This is followed by a discussion of the implications of these findings for sales management with emphasis on management practices that might improve salesperson job performance. Finally, ideas for further research are presented.

5.1 Summary of the Study

The study was based on a sample of 89 field salespeople from three firms. A self-report questionnaire probing the ways that the salespeople in the sample felt about issues such as their feelings toward various job related rewards and their perceptions concerning the relationships which might exist between the accomplishment of goals and the receipt of these job-related rewards. Also, information concerning the degree to which the salespeople feel that their job environments are "enriched", as well as information which deals in the salespersons' perceptions of the attributes of their tasks and goals, was solicited. Finally, each salesperson in the sample was asked to provide probabilistic "expectancy" figures in which his (her) own estimates of the "odds" that he would accomplish the goals which the company had set out for him, and also the "odds" that he would accomplish his own personal goals.

The sales manager questionnaire consisted of three different evaluations: a subjective measure of the overall sales performance of each salesperson in his territory, an objective measure of each salesperson's performance relative to quota standards set for him by his company, and a figure reflecting the sales volume which each salesperson is credited as having generated for the company.

The scales used in this study to evaluate the perceived degree of job enrichment and the attributes of the tasks and goals were evaluated for their reliability and were found to be within acceptable levels for behavioral research.

The results of the analyses concerning the four hypotheses which constitute the main part of this study were, except for Hypothesis Four, disconfirming to these hypotheses. Possible explanations for these results are given below.

5.1.1 Restriction of Range of Scores on "need Achievement"

One possible reason why the results were disconfirming for three of the four main hypotheses presented concerns the nature of the sample of salespersons used in this study. The members of this sample scored, on the whole, very high in the main construct used in this study: the need to achieve on the job. The "restriction of range" of "need Achievement" scores might mask a "need Achievement"-moderated relationship between either job scope or participation in quota-setting and sales performance, a relationship which would become evident if subjects exhibiting a wider range of "need Achievement" scores were used.

5.1.2 Job Enrichment Might Not be Motivationally Salient

Perhaps more compelling is the notion that the degree of enrichment of a sales job is just not a motivationally salient issue for the salespeople tested. Though the degree of enrichment which is possible in a job selling socks to retail department stores might be significantly less than the degree of enrichment which characterizes a position concerning the sale of space in freight containers, it does not necessarily follow that attempts should be made to increase the enrichment of the job selling socks. There appear to be very few ways that a given sales job can be significantly enriched, since the specific nature of the selling task appears to "lock" the selling position into a fairly rigid degree of "enrichment" which is possible. If one accepts this premise, then the salesperson who both accepts a sales position and stays in that position would probably not be motivationally sensitive to the scope of the job.

5.1.3 "Need Achievement" and "Expectancy" as the ONLY Performance Predictors

The present research indicates that, in line with the predictions of Lewin (1938), the motivational force on a salesperson to perform on the job is a function of two independent variables: the "push" of the need to achieve on the job, and the "pull" of the valent outcome which accomplishment of the salesperson's personal sales goal constitutes. The latter issue is motivationally salient for persons high in the need to achieve on the job.

A conceptual model which incorporates the empirical findings of this study and which represents a revision of the model presented in Chapter 1 is given in Figure 2.

Figure 2   A Revised Model of Salesperson Performance

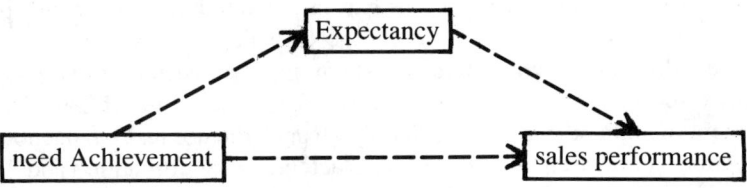

5.2   Management Implications

In this section, management implications of the regression analyses for management practices, procedures and policies are presented. These implications come under the categories of personnel selection procedures and management programs.

5.2.1   "Need Achievement" and Sales Personnel Selection

A prime criterion for selecting sales personnel should be the prospective salesperson's need to achieve on the job. Since studies show that a persons score on a "need Achievement" scale does not change much after the onset of puberty, the policies which are intended to affect a salesperson's need to achieve after he is hired may not have the intended effects. The most logical time to use information concerning a salesperson's need to achieve, then, is when the (prospective) salesperson is being considered for a sales position within the company. The higher the salesperson's need to achieve, the better prospect that he is for the sales position.

5.2.2   Management Programs and Salesperson Motivation

It appears that management programs such as "job enrichment" are not useful in improving sales performance. As was described previously, the kind of person who will take a given sales position and stay in that position is probably not motivationally sensitive to an aspect of the job—such as the degree of enrichment of the job—which is, basically, inflexible. In short, then, the sales manager need not be concerned with management programs such as "job enrichment" for improving the job performance of the salesforce.

5.3   Ideas for Further Research

Several ideas for further salesforce research in areas related to the ones discussed in this study appear to offer promise. These ideas are listed in the two sections which follow.

5.3.1 The Search for Useful Individual Difference Variables

The success which this researcher has had in predicting a salesperson's performance from his need to achieve leads one to believe that a search for other "individual difference" characteristics which might be correlated with superior sales performance would be in order. Three other "needs" which have received some attention in the context of predicting job performance and satisfaction from organizational climate are the "needs" for "autonomy", "affiliation" and "dominance". The initial search would be one wherein these constructs would be tested as either predictors of sales performance or as moderators between sales performance and constructs or construct sets such as the job enrichment variables.

5.3.2 Develop Taxonomies of Job Outcomes

In this study, the validity of a "process" model investigating the relationship between a salesperson's "valence for performance" composite and sales performance was tested, with non-confirming results coming from the tests. Perhaps a more fundamental step to take before one posits a process model of salesperson motivation would be to develop taxonomies of job outcomes for which high performing salespeople characteristically have a high valence. The results of this research can then be combined with the results of research alluded to in the first idea presented in this "Further Research" section. The result is that one can then better determine if a salesperson's "needs" (individual differences) and "valences" (for job outcomes) stem from a common source. If a common source is uncovered, then the heretofore separate literatures concerning the motivational importance of "needs" and "valences" can be combined under one framework, and the drive toward parsimony in devising theories of motivation, in general, and salesperson motivation, in particular, will have been carried one step further.

Appendix: Survey Materials

Advance Notice Letter from Management

Dear   :

    I wanted to bring your attention to an important project which is now underway in the company. We are undertaking a study and are very interested in your opinions and those of other sales representatives in the company. The basic objective of the study is to gain a better understanding of what motivates you to perform on the job. In this study, we will all be working with Nick Williamson, an expert in salesperson motivation from the University of North Carolina. I am attaching a letter from Mr. Williamson which provides some additional information about the study.

    An outside expert is directing this study to give you the opportunity to provide complete and frank inputs. Your responses will be in strict confidence to Mr. Williamson, and only he will have access to your individual responses. His report to the company will provide only statistical summary information and your individual responses will in no way be identifiable. We want it this way to insure and encourage your frank responses.

    The primary purpose of this letter is to let you know ahead of time that in the near future you will receive a questionnaire related to this project. Because the project is important to you and to the company, I am asking your complete and prompt cooperation in providing the information requested. The questionnaire is interesting, and I believe that you will enjoy thinking about the issues it raises.

    You will receive the questionnaire and directions in about two weeks. We are certain that all of our efforts on this project will be worthwhile. A better understanding of your attitudes about your job can help us all to develop a better and more supportive sales organization. Thank you in advance for your conscientious help.

Sincerely,

(Vice-President, Sales)

Advance Notice Letter from the Researcher

Dear

    I am most pleased that your company will be participating in the research study.

    The following is a brief summary of the proposed study. It is composed of several components on which data will be collected through the use of one complete survey questionnaire. In each component are items or questions which ask you for your feelings about various aspects of your job. Each component will be analyzed separately for its implications with respect your motivation to perform on the job. Additionally, each component will be compared with other components to determine which component is most important in determining your motivation and performance on the job. One component addresses how you feel about the various rewards which may stem from performing well on the job. Items in another component relate to specific aspects of the job environment that you work in, such as the feedback which you may receive from your first line supervisor, the variety of the tasks which you accomplish, and others. The last component addresses the process by which you and your supervisor develop your sales quota.

    Naturally, the frank and honest answers of your sales force are essential to the accuracy and value of the study. Of course, replies will remain confidential and will be used only in combination with responses from other salesmen participating in the study. There are several hundred salespersons from several firms involved, thus a particular individual's responses within a firm or among the aggregate will not be identifiable.

    After the study, corporate management will be provided a summary of the findings specific to the participating company, and a report aggregating all participants for purposes of comparison with the entire sample.

    I feel strongly that there will be very beneficial outcomes to both the sales force and sales management resulting from the study. I appreciate your cooperation and endorsement, and look forward to working with your sales force on this study.

                                                       Sincerely,

                                                  Nick Williamson

Letter from Company to Participants

Dear_____:

Enclosed is the questionnaire that I indicated would be forthcoming in my letter of_____. I would appreciate your conscientious and speedy completion of the questionnaire. This is an important undertaking in our company and we hope to be able to learn much about our sales force through our participation.

Would you please cooperate with the instruction given by Mr. Williamson to the fullest? I recognize the time that will be involved in completing the questionnaire (approximately 75 minutes), but encourage you to complete it within the next week. Please respond honestly and frankly. As I noted in my earlier letter, Mr. Williamson is an independent researcher conducting this study and your responses will remain in his confidence and anonymous to the company. With this approach, the information should be useful and enlightening to us all.

It is only through your cooperation and effort that we will all be able to benefit from this study. Please take the time to complete the questionnaire and forward it to Mr. Williamson as soon as possible. We should have some results to pass on to you by late summer or early fall.

Sincerely,

Cover Letter from the Researcher to the Salespersons

Dear Salesperson:

We are conducting, in cooperation with your company, a survey among sales professionals. This survey includes salespersons like yourself from among several industrial and consumer goods manufacturing firms who are providing information through a uniform questionnaire. Your responses to the statements in the questionnaire will enable your firm to better understand how its sales organization currently functions, the effects of its policies and procedures and other related topics on the motivation of its salesforce. Also, it will enable your company to examine characteristics of its sales organization with respect to other sales organizations.

We are counting on you to provide frank and accurate information in a conscientious manner. Your opinions are very important to this research and a significant contribution to the understanding of the selling profession can only result through your cooperation in completing the enclosed questionnaire.

The questionnaire is extensive, but such an approach is needed to obtain accurate measures of the many complex characteristics surrounding your job. Additionally, such an approach will permit an accurate analysis of the information provided by all participating firms. Your accuracy and completeness in responding to the questionnaire, therefore, are most important to the usefulness of the study to your firm, and ultimately to you.

Of course, your responses are confidential and will be used only in combination with those of other salespersons within your company; you will never be identified individually. However, it is important to maintain a record of who has returned completed questionnaires to insure a complete response. Thus, the following procedure will be used to insure both complete confidentiality and a complete response. After you have completed the questionnaire, please insert it in the pre-addressed envelope provided, seal the envelope, and in the space provided on the flap of the envelope print your name and the name of your company. Then simply mail the sealed package from your office. When it is received here at the University of North Carolina, your name will be checked off a master list as having returned the completed questionnaire, and the envelope with your identification will be destroyed. Thus, all of your responses will remain anonymous as their are no additional identifying marks on the questionnaire, but those who have not completed the questionnaire can be reminded to do so by their company. These extra procedures are being made to insure your anonymity and to fully encourage your frank, honest and complete response. Without such response, the study will not be useful to you, or to your company.

Your company will be receiving a report on the findings of this study (probably late summer or early fall) and it will be made available to you. We think that you will find that the questionnaire is provocative and interesting, and that it will afford you the opportunity to express your opinions about many important aspects of your job. Please make every effort to complete and return this questionnaire within the next week.

Your valuable effort and cooperation is very much appreciated. We are sure there will be significant benefits forthcoming to you and to your company through your conscientious effort in this research.

Sincerely,

Nick Williamson
Project Director

Letter from the Researcher to the Sales Manager

Dear Sales Manager:

We are conducting in cooperation with your company, a survey among sales professionals. This survey includes sales managers like yourself from several industrial and consumer goods manufacturing companies providing information through a uniform questionnaire. Your responses to statements in the questionnaire will enable your firm to better understand what motivates the members of its salesforce to perform on the job.

We are counting on you to provide frank and accurate information in a conscientious manner. Your opinions and objective assessments are extremely important to this research and a significant contribution to the understanding of the selling profession can only result through your cooperation in completing the enclosed questionnaire.

The questionnaire is extensive, but such an approach is needed to obtain accurate measures of the many complex characteristics surrounding the selling profession. Additionally, such an approach will permit an accurate analysis of the information provided by all participating firms. Your accuracy and completeness in responding to the questionnaire, therefore, are important to the usefulness of the study to your firm, and ultimately to yourself.

Of course, your responses are confidential and will be used only in combination with those other sales professionals within your company; you will never be identified individually. However, it is important to obtain a record of who has returned completed questionnaires to insure a complete response. Thus, the following procedure will be used to insure both confidentiality and a complete response. After you have completed the questionnaire, please insert it in the pre-addressed envelope and print your name and the name of your company. Then, simply mail the sealed package from your office. When it is received here at the University of North Carolina, your name will be checked off a master list as having returned the completed questionnaire, and the envelope with your identification will be destroyed. Thus, all of your responses will remain anonymous as there are no additional identifying marks on the questionnaire, but those who have not completed the questionnaire can be reminded to do so by their company. These extra procedures are being made to insure your anonymity and to fully encourage your frank, honest and complete response.

Your company will be receiving a report on the findings of this study (probably in late summer or early fall) and it will be made available to you. We think you will find the questionnaire to be interesting and will allow you to make some evaluations of the salespersons under you which you might not have had the opportunity to do before. Please make every effort to complete and return this questionnaire within the next week.

Your valuable effort and cooperation is very much appreciated. We are sure there will be significant benefits forthcoming to you and to your company through your conscientious effort in this research.

Sincerely,

Nick Williamson
Project Director

Determination of Quota Fulfillment Expectancies

INSTRUCTIONS: In this section, please consider the various Performance Targets that your COMPANY expects you to meet for the quarter beginning July 1, 1980 and ending September 30, 1980. Please assign probability figures giving your estimate of your chances that you will meet the Performance Targets. Please use the space provided below.

CATEGORY	PROBABILITY OF ACCOMPLISHMENT
Sales Calls to be Made	_____
Dozens of Product to be sold	_____
Brand extensions to be made	_____
New accounts to be acquired	_____
Fixtures to be sold	_____
Facings to be gained	_____
Displays to be sold or set	_____

Determination of Personal Sales Goal Probabilities

INSTRUCTIONS: In this section, please consider the various Performance Targets that you yourself PERSONALLY want to meet for the quarter beginning July 1, 1980 and ending September 30, 1980. Please assign probability figures giving your estimate of your chances that you will meet your OWN PERSONAL Targets. Please use the space provided below.

CATEGORY	PROBABILITY OF ACCOMPLISHMENT
Sales Calls to be Made	_____
Dozens of Product to be sold	_____
Brand extensions to be made	_____
New accounts to be acquired	_____
Fixtures to be sold	_____
Facings to be gained	_____
Displays to be sold or set	_____

Model Comparisons to be Used in Testing Job Scope Vars

—There are 6 independent (Job Scope) variables

—There are 2 dependent (Job Performance) variables

—There are 2 covariates (Valence for attaining Sales Quota and Valence for attaining Personal Sales Goal)

Dependent variables = $Y(i)$, $i = 1$ to 5

Independent variables = $X(k)$, $k = 3$ to 8

Covariates = $X(j), j = 1,2$

MODEL I(i): $Y(i) = B(i0) + B(i1) \times (1) + \ldots + B(i8) \times (8) + e$

MODEL II(i): $Y(i) = B(i0) + B(i1) \times (1) + B(i3) \times (3) + B(i4) \times (4) + \ldots + B(i8) \times (8) + e$

MODEL III(i): $Y(i) = B(i0) + B(i2) \times (2) + B(i3) \times (3) + \ldots + B(i8) \times (8) + e$

MODEL IV(i): $Y(i) = B(i0) + B(i3) \times (3) + B(i4) \times (4) + \ldots + B(i8) \times (8) + e$

Characteristics of the Scales to be Used

1. Job Scope scale

    Estimated reliabilities of the six descriptive dimensions

    (estimated internal consistencies)

DIMENSION	RATING
Variety	.86
Autonomy	.89
Task Identity	.95
Feedback	.97
Dealing with others	.88
Friendship opportunities	.92

Manifest Needs Questionnaire (MNQ)

   Reliability

   Test-retest—.72, .75, .77 and .86 for the four "need" scales

   Internal consistency—.66, .56, .61, and .83, for the four "need" scales, respectively.

Task-Attribute Goal Questionnaire(TGAQ)

   Internal Consistencies of the five scales:

   Using Cronbach's Alpha: Participation (.72), feedback (.81), peer competition (.69), goal specificity (.68) and goal difficulty (.72).

Bibliography

Adams, J. S. "Toward an Understanding of Inequity", *Journal of Abnormal and Social Psychology* (November, 1963) pp.422–436.
Alderfer, Clayton. *Existence, Relatedness and Growth*. (New York: Free Press, 1972)
Alport, Mark I. and Robert A. Peterson. "On the Interpretation of Canonical Analysis" *Journal of Marketing Research* Vol IX (May 1972) pp. 187–192.
Atkinson, John. *Motives in Fantasy, Action and Society*. Princeton, N. J.: Van Nostrand, 1958.
Atkinson, J. W. *An Introduction to Motivation* (Princeton, N. J., 1964).
―――― Some General Implications of Conceptual Developments in the Study of Achievement-Oriented Behavior, in M. R. Jones (ed.) *Human Motivation: A Symposium*. Lincoln, Neb.: University of Nebraska Press, 1965.
―――― and Joel O. Raynor (eds., 1974) *Motivation and Achievement*, New York: Halsted Press.
Bagozzi, R. P. *Toward a General Theory for the Explanation of the Performance of Salespeople* unpublished doctoral dissertation, Northwestern University, 1976.
―――― (1978) "Salesforce Performance and Satisfaction as a Function of Individual Difference, Interpersonal and Situational Factors," *Journal of Marketing Research*, Vol. XV (November) pp. 517–531.
―――― (1980), "Performance and Satisfaction in an Industrial Sales Force: An Examination of their Antecedents and Simultaneity," *Journal of Marketing*, Vol. 44 (Spring), pp. 65–77.
Barr, Anthony J., et al *A User's Guide to SAS 76* (Raleigh, N. C.: SAS Institute, 1976).
Bass, Frank M. and William L. Wilkie "A Comparative Analysis of Attitudinal Prediction of Brand Preference" *Journal of Marketing Research* Vol X, August 1973, pp. 262–269.
Behrman, Douglas and Perreault, William D., Jr. "Measuring the Performance of Industrial Salespersons", Working Paper, UNC-Chapel Hill, December 1978.
Bem, Daryl J. *Beliefs, Attitudes and Human Affairs*. Belmont, Calif.: Brooks/Cole, 1970.
Beswick, C. A. and D. W. Cravens "A Multi-Stage Model for Salesforce Management", *Journal of Marketing Research* XIV (May 1977), pp. 135–144.
Black, R. W. Incentive Motivation and the Parameters of Reward in Instrumental Conditioning. In J. W. Arnold and D. Levine (eds.) *Nebraska Symposium on Motivation* Lincoln: University of Nebraska Press, 1969.
Bock, Darrel. *Multivariate Statistical Methods in Behavioral Research*. (New York: McGraw-Hill Book Company, 1975).
Calder, B. J. and B. M. Staw, "The Interaction of Intrinsic and Extrinsic Motivation: Some Methodological Notes" *Journal of Personality and Social Psychology* 31: pp. 76–80 (1975).
Campbell, John P., Marvin D. Dunnette, Edward E. Lawler, III and Karl E. Weick, Jr. *Managerial Behavior, Performance and Effectiveness*. New York: McGraw-Hill, 1970.
Campbell, J. P. and R. D. Pritchard (1976), "Motivational Theory in Industrial and Organizational Psychology," In Marvin D. Dunnette (eds.), *Handbook of Industrial and Organizational Psychology*. Chicago: Rand-McNally.

Churchill, Gilbert A. Jr. "Linear Attitude Models: A Study of Predictive Ability", *Journal of Marketing Research* IX (November 1972), pp. 423–425.

———— Neil M. Ford and Orville C. Walker, Jr. "Measuring the Job Satisfaction of Industrial Salesmen", *Journal of Marketing Research* XI (August 1974) pp. 254–260.

———— Neil M. Ford and Orville C. Walker, Jr. "Organizational Climate and Satisfaction in the Salesforce", *Journal of Marketing Research* XIII (November 1976) pp. 323–332.

Cotham, James C., III. "Selecting Salesmen: Approaches and Problems" *MSU Business Topics* Vol 18, Winter 1970, pp. 64–72.

Cramer, Elliot M. "Significance Tests and Tests of Models in Multiple Regression", *The American Statistician*. October 1972, Vol. 26, No. 4.

Cravens, D. W. and R. B. Woodruff. "An Approach for Determining Criteria of Sales Performance", *Journal of Applied Psychology*. 57 (1973), pp. 240–247.

———— R. B. Woodruff and J. C. Stamper "An Analytical Approach for Evaluating Sales Territory Performance", *Journal of Marketing* Vol. 36 (January 1972), pp. 31–37.

Dachler, H. P. and W. H. Mobley, "Construct Validation of an Instrumentality-Expectancy Task-Goal Model of Work Motivation: Some Theoretical Boundary Conditions", *Journal of Applied Psychology* (1973), 58, pp. 397–418.

Darmon, Renee. "Salesmen's Response to Financial Incentives: An Empirical Study", *Journal of Marketing Research* XI (November 1974), pp. 418–426.

Davis, Kenneth R. and Frederick E. Webster, Jr. *Sales Force Management*. (New York: The Ronald Press, 1968).

De Charms, M. *Annual Review of Psychology, 1978*.

Deci, E. L. *Intrinsic Motivation*. New York: Plenum, 1975.

Donnelly, James, James Gibson and John Ivancevich. *Fundamentals of Management*. (Dallas: Business Publications, Inc., 1975).

Doyle, Steven and Irving Shapiro. "How to Motivate Your Salesforce", *Harvard Business Review*. May–June 1980.

Drucker, Peter F. *The Practice of Management*. (New York: Harper and Row, 1954).

Dyer, Lee and Donald F. Parker. "Classifying Outcomes in Work Motivation Research: An Examination of the Intrinsic-Extrinsic Dichotomy", *Journal of Applied Psychology*. 1975, Vol. 60, No. 4, pp. 455–458.

Etzel, Michael J. and John M. Ivancevich. "Management by Objectives in Marketing: Philosophy, Process and Problems", *Journal of Marketing*. October 1974, Vol. 38, #4, pp. 47–55.

Festinger, Leon. *A Technical Study of Some Changes in Attitudes and Values Following Promotion in General Electric*. Crotonville, N. Y.: Behavioral Research Service, 1964.

Fishbein, Martin. "Attitude and the Prediction of Behavior", in Martin Fishbein, ed., *Readings in Attitude Theory and Measurement*. New York: John Wiley and Sons, 1967, pp. 447–492.

Futrell, Charles M., John E. Swan and Charles W. Lamb. "Benefits and Problems in a Salesforce MBO System", *Industrial Marketing Management*. 6 (1977), pp. 265–272.

Galbraith, J. and Cummings, L. "An Empirical Investigation of the Motivational . . . ", *Organizational Behavior and Human Performance*. 1967, 2.

Ghiselli, Edwin E. "The Validity of Aptitude Tests in Personnel Selection", *Personnel Psychology*. 26 (Winter 1973), pp. 461–477.

Gibson, James, John Ivancevich and James Donnelly, *Organizations* (Dallas: Business Publications, Inc., 1976).

Goodman, P. S. and A. Friedman, "An Examination of Adams' Theory of Inequity", *Administrative Science Quarterly* (December, 1971), pp. 271–288.

Graen, G. "Instrumentality Theory and Work Motivation: Some Experimental Results and Suggested Modifications", *Journal of Applied Psychology—Monograph*. (1969) 23, pp. 1–25.

Guzzo, R. A. "Types of Rewards, Cognitions and Work Motivation", *Academy of Management Review*. 1979, 4, pp. 75–86.

Hackman, J. R. and E. E. Lawler, III. "Employee Reaction to Job Characteristics", *Journal of Applied Psychology*. 1971, 55, pp. 259–286.

Hackman, J. R. and G. R. Oldham (1976), "Motivation Through the Design of Work: Test of a Theory," *Organizational Behavior and Human Performance*, Vol. 16, 250–279.

Hackman, J. R. and L. W. Porter "Expectancy Theory Predictions of Work Effectiveness", *Organizational Behavior and Human Performance* 1968, 3, pp. 417–426.

Hall, D. T. and K. E. Nougaim, "An Examination of Maslow's Need Hierarchy in an Organizational Setting", *Organizational Behavior and Human Performance* 1968, 3, pp. 12–35.

Hansen, F. "Consumer Choice Behavior: An Experimental Approach", *Journal of Marketing Research*. VI (1969), pp. 436–443.

Haring, Albert and Robert H. Myers. "Special Incentives for Salesmen", *Journal of Marketing*. 18 (October 1953), pp. 155–159.

Heneman, H. G., III and D. P. Schwab. "An Evaluation of Research on Expectancy Theory Predictions of Employee Performance", *Psychological Bulletin*. 1972, 78, pp. 1–9.

Herzberg, F., Mausner, B. and Snyderman, B. *The Motivation to Work*. (New York: John Wiley and Sons, 1959).

Hull, C. L. *A Behavior System* New Haven: Yale University Press, 1952.

Ivancevich, John M. "Changes in Performance in a MBO Program", *Administrative Science Quarterly*. 19 (1974) pp. 563–574.

Jackson, D. N. *Personality Research Form Manual*. (Goshen, N. Y.: Research Psychologists Press, 1967).

Jacoby, Jacob. "Consumer and Industrial Psychology: Prospects for Construct Validation and Mutual Contribution", in Marvin D. Dunnette, ed., *The Handbook of Industrial and Organizational Psychology*. (Chicago: Rand-McNally, 1976).

Jacobs, R. and T. Soloman (1977), "Strategies for Enhancing the Prediction of Job Performance from Job Satisfaction," *Journal of Applied Psychology*., Vol. G2, 417–421.

Jackson, Donald W. and Ramon D. Aldag. "Managing the Salesforce by Objectives", *MSU Business Topics*. V. 22, #2, Spring 1974, pp. 53–58.

Johnson, Stephen C. "Hierarchical Clustering Schemes", *Psychometrika*. XXXII (1967) pp. 241–254.

Jones, M. R. *Nebraska Symposium on Motivation* (Lincoln, Neb.: University of Nebraska Press, 1955).

Korman, A. K. (1970) "Toward an Hypothesis of Work Behavior," *Journal of Applied Psychology*, 54, pp. 31–41.

Latham, Gary P. and Gary A. Yukl. "A Review of the Research on the Application of Goal-Setting in Organizations", *Academy of Management Journal*. 18 (1975) pp. 824–845.

Lawler, E. E. *Motivation in Work Organizations*. Belmont, Calif.: Brooks/Cole, 1973.

Lawler, Edward E., III and J. L. Suttle. "A Causal Correlational Test of the Need Hierarchy Concept", *Organizational Behavior and Human Performance*. (1972) pp. 265–287.

Lewin, Kurt. *The Conceptual Representation and the Measurement of Psychological Forces*. (Durham, N. C.: Duke University Press, 1938).

Litwin, G. H. and R. A. Stringer. *Motivation and Organizational Climate*. Boston: Division of Research, Graduate School of Business Administration, Harvard University, 1968.

Locke, E. A., "Toward a Theory of Task Motivation and Incentives", *Organizational Behavior and Performance* (1968), 3, pp. 157–189.

——— "The Ubiquity of the Techniques of Goal-Setting in Theories and Approaches to Employee Motivation", *Academy of Management Review*. 1978 (July).

——— Cartledge, N. and Knerr, C. S., "Studies of the Relationship between Satisfaction, Goal-Setting and Performance", *Organizational Behavior and Human Performance*, 1970, 5, pp. 135–158.

Lucas, Henry C., Charles B. Weinberg and Kenneth W. Clowes. "Sales Response as a Function of Territory Potential and Sales Representative Workload", *Journal of Marketing Research*. Vol. XII (August 1975), pp. 298–305.

Maslow, Abraham. *Motivation and Personality*. (New York: Harper and Row, 1954).
McClelland, David C., et. al. *The Achievement Motive*. (New York: Irvington Publishers, 1976).
McGregor, Douglas. "An Uneasy Look at Performance Appraisal", *Harvard Business Review* 35 pp. 74–89 (1957).
———— *The Human Side of Enterprise*. New York: McGraw-Hill, 1960).
Meyer, H. H., E. Kay and J. R. P. French, Jr., "Split Roles Performance Appraisal", *Harvard Business Review* 1965, 43 (1), pp. 123–129.
Mitchell, Terrence R. (1974), "Expectancy Models of Satisfaction, Occupational Preference and Effort: A Theoretical, Methodological and Empirical Appraisal," *Psychological Bulletin*, Vol. 891, 1053–1077.
Murray, H. A. *Exploration into Personality*. (New York: Oxford University Press, 1938).
Nicosia, F. M. *Consumer Decision Processes* Englewood Cliffs, N. J.: Prentice-Hall, 1966.
Nunnally, J. C. (1967), *Psychometric Theory*. New York: McGraw-Hill.
Oliver, Richard. "Expectancy Theory Predictions of Salesmen's Performance", *Journal of Marketing Research*. Vol. XI (August 1974), pp. 243–253.
Opsahl, Robert L. and Marvin D. Dunnette, "The Role of Financial Compensation in Industrial Motivation" *Psychological Bulletin*, 66 (August 1966), pp. 94–118.
Parker, Donald F. and Lee Dyer. "Expectancy Theory as a Within-Person Behavioral Choice Model: An Empirical Test of Some Conceptual and Methodological Refinements", *Organizational Behavior and Human Performance*. 17 (1976), pp. 97–117.
Porter, L. W. and E. E. Lawler, III. *Managerial Attitudes and Performance*. (Homewood, Ill.: Dorsey Press, 1968).
Perreault, William D., Jr. and Rosann Spiro. "An Approach for Improved Interpretation of Multivariate Analysis", *Decision Sciences*. Vol. 9, No. 3 (July 1978).
Pritchard, R. D. and B. W. Karasick. "The Effects of Organizational Climate on Managerial Job Performance and Satisfaction", *Organizational Climate and Human Performance*. 1973, 9, pp. 126–146.
Pritchard, R. D. and M. S. Sanders, "The Influence of Valence Instrumentalities and Expectancy on Effort and Performance", *Journal of Applied Psychology*, 1973, 57, pp. 55–60.
Pruden, Henry O., William H. Cunningham and Wilke D. English. "Non-financial Incentives for Salesmen", *Journal of Marketing*. October 1972, pp. 55–59.
Raia, Anthony P. "A Second Look at Management Goals and Controls", *California Management Review*. 8 (1964), pp. 49–58. bib. Rosenberg, Milton J. "Cognitive Structure and Attitudinal Effort", *Journal of Abnormal and Social Psychology*. 53 (November 1956), pp. 367–372.
Ryans, Adrian B. and Charles B. Weinberg. "Determinants of Sales Force Performance: A Multiple Company Study", Working Paper, Graduate School of Business, Stanford University, July 1978.
Schmidt, F. L., "Implications of a Measurement Problem for Expectancy Theory Research", *Organizational Behavior and Human Performance*, 1973, 10, pp. 243–251.
Scott, Jerome E. and Peter D. Bennett. "Cognitive Models of Attitude Structure: Value Importance IS Important", *Proceedings*. Fall Conference, AMA, 1971, pp. 346–350.
Sheth, Jagdish and W. Wayne Talarzyk. "Perceived Instrumentality and Value Importance as Determinants of Attitudes", *Journal of Marketing Research*. IX (February 1972), pp. 6–9.
Skinner, B. F. *Beyond Freedom and Dignity*. New York: Knopf, 1971.
Smyth, Richard. "Financial Incentives for Salesmen", *Harvard Business Review*. January-February, 1968, pp. 109–117.
Stanton, William J. and Richard H. Buskirk. *Management of the Sales Force*. (Homewood, Ill.: Richard D. Irwin, 1969).
Stedry, A. C. and E. Kay. *The Effects of Goal Difficulty on Performance*. General Electric Behavioral Research Services, 1966.

Steers, Richard M. "Task-Goal Attributes Achievement, N and Supervisory Performance", *Organizational Behavior and Human Performance*. 13 (1975), pp. 392–403.
_____ "Factors Affecting Job Attitudes in a Goal-Setting Environment", *Academy of Management Journal*. 19 (1976), pp. 6–16.
_____ and D. N. Braunstein. "A Behaviorally-Based Measure of Manifest Needs in Work Settings", *Journal of Vocational Behavior*. 9 (1976), pp. 251–266.
_____ and Lyman Porter. *Motivation and Work Behavior*.
_____ and Daniel G. Spencer. "The Role of Achievement Motivation in Job Design", *Journal of Applied Psychology*. 1977, Vol. 62, No. 4, pp. 472–479.
Still, Richard R. and Edward W. Cundiff. *Sales Management*. Second Edition, (Englewood Cliffs, N. J.: Prentice-Hall, 1969).
Taylor, Frederick W. *Scientific Management*. (New York: Harper and Row, 1911).
Vroom, Victor. *Work and Motivation*. (New York: John Wiley and Sons, 1964).
Walker, Orville E., Jr., Gilbert A. Churchill, Jr., and Neil M. Ford. "Motivation and Performance in Industrial Selling: Present Knowledge and Needed Research", *Journal of Marketing Research*. XIV (May 1977), pp. 156–168.
Whitsett, D. A. and E. K. Winslow, "An Analysis of Studies Critical to the Motivation-Hygiene Theory", *Personnel Psychology* (1967) pp. 391–416.
Wilkie, William L. and Edgar A. Pessemier. "Issues in Marketing's Use of Multi-Attribute Attitude Models", *Journal of Marketing Research*. X (November 1973), pp. 428–441.
Williams, W. E. and D. A. Seiler, "A Relationship between Measure of Effort and Job Performance", *Journal of Applied Psychology*, 1973, 57, pp. 49–54.
Winer, B. J. *Statistical Principles in Experimental Design*. Second Edition. (New York: McGraw-Hill Book Co., 1971).
Winer, Leon (1973), "The Effect of Product Sales Quotas on Sales Force Productivity," *Journal of Marketing Research*, Vol. X (May), 180–183.
Young, James R. and Robert W. Mondy. *Personal Selling: Function, Theory and Practice*. (Hinsdale, Ill.: Dryden Press, 1978).

Index

Adam's Three-Step Equity Theory, 20-21
Aldefer's ERG Theory, 29-30
Atkinson's Need Achievement Theory, 31-32

goal setting
    as predictor of motivation and performance, 9-10
    comparison with Atkinson and Vroom, 14
    expectancy theory, 34, 109

Herzberg's Theory of Satisfiers and Dissatisfiers, 28-29
Hull's Drive Theory, 18-19

job challenge
    as predictor of motivation and performance, 1, 9-10
    job goal and need achievement, 10
job enrichment
    effects of, 14, 17
    implications for management, 113
    limitations, 112
    motivational receptivity, 30
    need achievement, 31-32
    on motivation and performance, 6-8
    performance composite, 87-88
    validity of application, 2
job environment, 6-7
job outcome
    analysis, 47-50, 58
    hypothesis on motivation, 38, 93, 95-101
    Vroom's Theory, 6, 21
job scope
    analysis, 50-51
    as predictor of motivation and performance, 1-2, 6-7
    effects of, 13-14
    intercorrelations among VIE constructs and MBO variables, 89-90
    models used in testing, 121
    need achievement, 85
    variables listed, 43, 66-69, 90

Law of Effect
    expectancy and, 109
    implications of, 24
    properties of, 24
Lewin's Field Theory, 19

Management by Objectives (MBO)
    fundamental steps, 7-8
    intercorrelations with VIE and MPS variables, 89-90
    need achievement, 31-32
    salesperson motivation, 8
    strength of system, 8
    task-goal attributes, 32-34, 43, 89-90
    validity of application, 2
    viability of, 14
Maslow's Theory of Need Hierarchy, 29
methodology
    collecting procedure, 36
    measurement and scales, 40-43
    sample letters for study, 115-20
    sampling procedure, 35
    sample questions, 120-21
    summary of, 111-12
motivation and performance
    calculation of force score, 4, 40
    drawback of content theories on, 31
    expectancy, 5, 20-21, 23-24, 27
    implications for management, 2
    job design, 33
    job enrichment, 112
    job performance and goals, 85
    job performance and need achievement, 51-52
    Law of Effect, 24
    MBO system, 8-9
    measurement of, 44-47
    model for predicting, 12-13
    money as motivator, 16
    need achievement, 9, 32, 85
    participation process and job autonomy, 88-89

130   Index

performance variables and VIE constructs, 48, 87-88, 112-13
Vroom's Theory, 3-7, 21-28
motivation theories
   content and process theories, 15-16, 19-31, 32
   Drive Theory, 18-19
   ERG Theory, 29-30
   Field Theory, 19
   human relations, 17
   need achievement, 31-32
   need hierarchy, 29
   reinforcement, 17-18
   satisfiers and dissatisfiers, 28-29
   scientific management, 16-17
   Three-step Equity Theory, 20-21

need achievement
   as predictor for motivation and performance, 1, 6-7, 112-13
   definition of, 31-32
   determines expectancy, 31-32, 38, 51-52, 94, 105-109
   goal setting, 9-10
   hypothesis of job scope and job performance, 38, 93-95, 101
   hypothesis on participation in goal setting and job performance, 38, 51-52, 99, 102-6
   implications for management, 113
   job design, 33
   job scope, 85
   measurement of, 43, 52, 74, 112
   motivation receptivity to job enrichment, 31
   participation and autonomy variables, 89
   predictions from Atkinson's Theory, 11
   relationship between performance and, 3, 86-87
   relationship between task-goal attributes and, 34, 85
   variables tested, 43, 91

performance variables, 91-92

rewards
   affecting nature of motivation, 23
   as predictor of motivation and performance, 6

Skinner's Reinforcement Theory, 17-18

task-goal attribute
   as hypothesis variable, 1-2, 43, 89-90
   as predictor of motivation and performance, 9-10
   effects of, 13-14
   job or task challenge, 9-10
   MBO, 89-90
   need achievement, 85
   work motivation, 33
Taylor, Frederick
   influence of, 3, 6
   theory of motivation, 16

valence, instrumentality and expectancy (VIE)
   as seen in Equity Theory, 20-21
   "between person's" model, 1, 4-5, 13
   constructs measured, 40-43
   empirical problems, 24
   intercorrelations among MBO and MPS variables, 89-90
   measurement problems, 25-27
   performance variables and, 87
   refinements of measurement of, 1
Vroom's Theory
   as a process theory, 21
   as a "between person's" model, 1, 23
   as a predictor of motivation and performance, 2-4
   as a "within person's" model, 4-5, 23
   comparison with Atkinson and Locke, 14
   expectancy variable, 23-24, 31
   measurement issues, 5, 10, 25-26
   problems with misspecification, measurement and control factors, 22-24, 25-27